T0064161

=== *A Handbook for* ===

FIRST TIME MANAGERS

*Critical Pointers That New Managers
Need to Know to Succeed in Their Managerial Role*

Salwana Ali

PARTRIDGE
A Penguin Random House Company

To order additional copies of this book, contact
Toll Free 800 101 2657 (Singapore)
Toll Free 1 800 81 7340 (Malaysia)
orders.singapore@partridgepublishing.com

www.partridgepublishing.com/singapore

To all aspiring first time managers

Contents

PREFACE

THE GOALS OF THIS BOOK are two folds. First is to create awareness of the exact demands of the managerial role. Second is to help aspiring first time managers prepare for their new roles.

I decided to write this book after years of observation during the course of my work on how first time managers have struggled in their roles. They struggled to make informed decisions, solve problems in a timely manner, manage individual and team performances, build relationships and set directions.

Many underestimated the work scope of managers. Being such high achievers and accomplished individuals (typically the reason why they got promoted in the first place), they walked into the roles fully confident that they would have performed as well, if not better. Little did they know that the managerial roles demand very different skill sets. They ended up learning the skills and adapting to the new changes by trial and error, learning on the job. Some got through well and some did not.

Their lack of awareness and readiness resulted in unnecessary bottlenecks that hurt the efficiency and effectiveness of the organizations. A new sales manager operating in his comfort zone for instance, would be inclined to still prospect and meet potential clients rather than setting directions and helping his team members secure resources and solve problems. In tough situations, his inability to analyze complex problems and make sound decision can lead to life changing experiences for the people he managed. Both scenarios proved costly to organizations and should be avoided.

It typically takes between six to twelve months for first time managers to learn the ropes of being managers. In developing this book, I spoke to many friends, colleagues, ex-colleagues, clients and business associates who have had successful careers in general management.

Our discussions started with a key question, "what were your real life experiences when you became a manager for the first time?" Based on these findings I established a common theme of scenarios which I categorized into four evolutionary stages: Honeymoon, Reality, Readjustment and Coming Together.

Next, I worked further on a second key question, "how can first time managers be ready from day one on the job?" While the degree of readiness may vary among the new managers, the key principle is to provide awareness on the demands of the role and the most critical behavioural skills that they need to have. The outcome of the second question helped me to establish the cornerstones of the managerial role, a basis that all aspiring first time managers need to understand well to prepare themselves.

Organizations rely on continuous improvement to thrive and stay relevant. Hence, aspiring first time managers will need continuous assessment on their own performances. I established the third key question, "what types of tools are suitable for the first time managers to perform personal assessments on their own performances?" The outcome of this is a self-diagnostic tool that I created entitled The Manager's Toolkits.

The book is structured into two parts. Part 1: The Managerial Role describes the cornerstones of the managerial role, the environment that new managers operate in and the challenges faced by new managers. Part 2: The Manager's Toolkits describe the assessment tools that first time managers can use to self-diagnose their performances and take corrective actions as they see fit.

Any names mentioned in the real life examples in this book are fictitious as I respect the confidentiality understanding that I have established with the sources. I used the references of "he" and "his" in this book to reflect both genders.

I believe that all managers can benefit from this book. While first time managers and current individual contributors who plan to become managers in the near future will benefit the most, middle managers will also benefit especially from The Manager's Toolkits, as the self-diagnostic assessment tools can be used by any managers to take stock on their performances at any point in time.

I sincerely hope that you will find this book helpful in your journey to become good managers. I wish you success in your management career.

Salwana Ali
Kuala Lumpur, Malaysia

ACKNOWLEDGEMENTS

I WOULD LIKE TO ACKNOWLEDGE THE contribution of many people in the development of this book. I am especially grateful to Dato' Dr Faridah Ismail who has patiently spent many nights reading and editing my work. My special appreciation goes to Rozana Meili Abdullah for providing invaluable advice in the early formation of this book.

I thank the supportive readers and appreciate all the feedback which has helped immensely in the final outcome of this work: Benedict Lee, Yasmin Mahmood, Nor Azlin Zainal Abidin, Dr Cordelia Mason, See Lay Hong, Lisa Lam, Roszita Abu Hassan, Azizah Ali, Che Haniza Zakariya, Fadzidah Rashid, Mastura Ishak, Nor Zaida Abdul Talib, Mastura Mansor, Azlina Mohd Ariff, Azni Hassan Basri, Zuraina Abdul Majid, Roswati Abdul Ghani, Faridah Yushak, Raja Azam Baeizah and Ruhaidah Shamsuddin.

A special thanks to my mother who has been my true inspiration.

INTRODUCTION

IF AND WHEN YOU PLAN to be a manager, take time to understand your personal motivations for wanting to be one. Different people may have different reasons for wanting to be a manager. The reasons can be, but not limited to, the following:

- To advance a career to the next milestone.
- To have new, exciting and interesting challenges.
- To make a difference by providing greater contribution to an organization.
- To learn new skills in managing people.

Upon understanding your personal motivations, you will be in a good position to assess your readiness to undertake the role of a manager. The next step is to answer the following questions honestly:

- "Am I ready to be a manager?"
- "How will I know if I am ready for the role?"

The above is a very simple exercise that will help you determine your level of readiness to take the managerial role. As a manager, you will be the nucleus of your department. You are responsible and accountable to hold everything together. You orchestrate various teams and stakeholders to work together for a common purpose. You help your team members to solve problems. You coach and guide them to do the right things for the benefit of your organization. You negotiate with your peers to secure resources. In fact you have to do multiple roles effectively in a consistent manner to achieve the desired results for your organization.

Failing to do these roles effectively, will undoubtedly, bring detrimental consequences to your organization, your team members and yourself. Your organization may not be able to achieve the revenue or profit it aims for. Your people may be disillusioned of not having clear directions. They may end up doing a lot of things without clear results. In the end, they may quit on you. And as a result you may feel like a failure and end up losing confidence in your own ability to do good work. It is a vicious cycle that will hurt everyone in the long term.

It is important for you to understand that the role of a manager represents a major shift in how you work to achieve results. As an individual contributor, you are responsible and accountable for your own personal results. You are independent and have a high degree of control on the activities and the outcomes that you desire. On the other hand, a manager has to depend on others for excellent execution to achieve superb results. This requires tremendous skills of orchestrating, negotiating, motivating, coaching, guiding and many others in order to steer everyone towards the same direction.

Moving from an individual contributor to a manager involves a great deal of changes that you must be ready to embrace and adapt to be successful. A certain level of change management has to take place. You have to conduct your own personal change management to successfully aid the transition from an individual contributor to a manager.

Part 1: The Managerial Role

This section details out the cornerstones of the managerial role, the environment that managers operate in and key challenges that managers are commonly faced with.

The cornerstones of the managerial role will help you determine whether you are ready to be a manager. Here is the list of the four cornerstones:

- Cornerstone 1: Scope of being a manager
- Cornerstone 2: Function of leadership and management
- Cornerstone 3: Behavioural skills
- Cornerstone 4: Managing change

Approach it from the standpoint of self evaluation. For each cornerstone, identify where you feel you are and determine the next steps to further prepare you for the role.

The scope of being a manager is the first key cornerstone. First time managers must be aware of the exact scope of being a manager. While a job description of a manager may have details about the job, the "real world" of management is not as straight forward as it is on paper. The common themes of real life managers' experiences will set the tone for the exact scope of being a manager. The four evolutionary stages of being a manager will help you visualize what the role entails and set the right expectations.

The first stage, *Honeymoon*, is what the first time managers experience in their initial weeks on the job. At this stage they are excited about their new role. They are elated with the new sense of power and authority that they perceive they are entitled to. They think that the title of managers will drive commitment and obedience from their subordinates. Some may experience a longer honeymoon period than others which is highly dependent on their own situations in their environment. The key is managers should consider avoiding too long a honeymoon period to enhance their chances to be successful earlier rather than later.

The second stage is *Reality*. First time managers will be overwhelmed by the real demand of their roles earlier than they expect. They typically experience this after a few weeks on the job and this will go on for months. Some will start to take stock of where they stand when they hear feedback, indirectly as well as directly, about their performances.

The third stage is *Readjustment*. Those who take their performance feedback seriously will start doing something different in order to improve themselves. They reset their approaches and introduce new ways of working with their subordinates and stakeholders. This typically happens after five to six months on the job.

The fourth stage, *Coming Together*, is the time when the new managers settle in with the role. They are able to discharge authority and secure buy-ins from their team members as a result of the actions executed in the third stage. They are ready to lead.

The second key cornerstone is the **understanding of leadership and management**. It is important to distinguish the functions of leadership and management as they are not the same. The reality is managers need to perform both functions. They can only do this effectively when they have clarity on the distinctive functions of each.

The third key cornerstone is **behavioural skills** for managers. It is imperative that first time managers have the awareness on how success looks like. For instance, the success criteria of one manager may include high morale among his subordinates, growth of new product by 5% and increased business from repeat customers. In order to be successful, he has to understand what's required of him, his subordinates, his departmental processes and many other elements that will contribute to his success. However, the most basic foundation relies on his behavioural skills to orchestrate and integrate people, process and systems to work together. Focusing on these variables at the onset will help him deliberately prioritize on things that really matter, which in turn will enhance his chance to succeed in his roles.

The fourth key cornerstone is **managing change**. First time managers must be aware that they are embarking on a new territory confined by new rules. They are expected to produce results through people. They are responsible and accountable to the success of their subordinates. They have to be flexible and adaptable to play multiple roles such as negotiators, problem solvers, coaches, mentors, arbitrators, decision makers at any time required. This represents a major shift in work style and approach that new managers must adopt.

Part 2: The Manager's Toolkits

The Manager's Toolkits help first time managers build their own managerial plan roadmap. In addressing the question, "Am I ready to be a manager?" the toolkits provides a platform for aspiring first time managers to prepare themselves to be ready for the role.

The Manager's Toolkits consist of two key components: the *imManager Framework* and the *imManager Guide*. They work hand-in-glove together.

The *imManager Framework* is the diagnostic execution plan on how to approach the role of managers. The *imManager Guide* supports the execution plan by providing a list of questionnaires that will form the base for aspiring first time managers to assess where they are and develop their own personal managerial plan accordingly.

Using this Book

You will gain the most benefit by reading it in the current order of sequences especially so for individual contributors preparing to be managers and first time managers. At the end of each chapter in Part 1, there is a section entitled "Action Items for New Managers". I encourage you to execute the suggested action items. Apply them in your work daily. I am confident that you will reap the benefits gradually. For experienced middle managers interested to perform personal assessments on where they are or how well they are doing, they can proceed to Part 2 directly.

PART 1

The Managerial Role

THE KEY CORNERSTONES OF THE MANAGERIAL ROLE

W HAT ENTAILS GOOD MANAGEMENT? THE answer to this question can be many. Some of them are achieving the desired results within the stipulated timeframe, high performing team members, high morale among employees, satisfied customers, satisfied business partners, effective team work and excellent customer service. The list doesn't stop there. However, the common criterion shared by them is that they are the outcomes of "something great that happened deliberately" or good management, definitely not by chance.

While good management requires tight integration among people, process and systems in organizations, it is imperative for first time managers to understand its key cornerstones. The key cornerstones focus entirely on the managers themselves. These are variables within the managers' controls which they can readily influence the outcomes. The better control they have on these variables, the better managers they become. The key cornerstones of the managerial role as depicted in Diagram 1, are:

- Scope of being a manager
- Function of leadership and management
- Behavioural skills
- Managing change

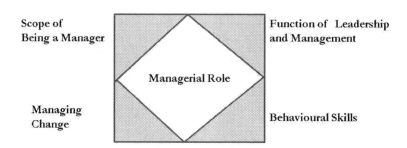

Diagram 1: Key Cornerstones of Managerial Role

CORNERSTONE 1:
THE SCOPE OF BEING A MANAGER

T HE BEST WAY TO UNDERSTAND the scope of being a manager is to view it from these perspectives:

- Perspective 1: To learn from the real life experiences of other managers.
- Perspective 2: To understand the environment that managers typically operate in.
- Perspective 3: To understand the key challenges faced by new managers.

Perspective 1: Real Life Experiences of New Managers

The experiences of first time managers in their first twelve months can be summarized into four key stages:

- Honeymoon

- Reality
- Readjustment
- Coming together

Stage 1: Honeymoon

The first time managers embrace the managerial role with excitement as this is a key milestone in their careers, a validation that they have done their jobs well and they have broken through to the next phase of their careers.

At this point in time, they perceive the role as glamorous and powerful. Since they have the title of "manager", they assume that they have formal authority as a "boss". They have the inclination to make decisions and be responsible for people, though they are not sure how that can be executed effectively. They believe that with the title of "manager", they will be able to do that easily as their team members are supposed to adhere to such protocol. They feel that they are entitled to such authority.

Many believe that they can perform better than their predecessors. They are confident that they are ready for the role. After all they had excellent track records when they were individual contributors, prior to their promotions.

In the beginning, they do not have much awareness that they are going through a "change" process, changing from an individual contributor to become people manager. As a result they function in the same way, operating in their own comfort zones and to their strengths. The new managers will get very bogged down quickly and stressed by the amount of work that they need to do.

At this point in time, their subordinates are just observing on how their new managers function. Oftentimes, they are very sceptical about their managers. They feel unsettled as they are not sure whether their new managers can add value to them. And more importantly, they are not convinced that their new managers have their interests at heart, until proven otherwise.

Stage 2: Reality

A few weeks into the job, many end up being so overwhelmed by the amount of work and the pace of everything around them.

As an example, Johan's real life experiences are included from this stage onwards to illustrate the complex situations that many new managers face. Johan recalled in his first few weeks as a first time manager,

> "I got so overwhelmed by the demand of the managerial role even in my first couple of weeks. When I came on board I had five big outstanding cases left by my predecessor that I needed to sort out. In addition, I had six direct reports with varied experiences. Two of them joined the company the same time as I did. I had a feeling that they were dejected by my promotion as in a way we grew up learning things together. Maybe they felt they deserved the promotion more than I. Then, I had two other direct reports who were average performers. One direct report was a new employee and the final one was a little problematic. I spent my time just fire fighting, trying to resolve issues that my direct reports had and they had plenty every day. I remember spending a lot more time with my average performers. I followed them to see clients, helped them in their planning sessions. That went on for a while as I felt that I was adding real value. I was very comfortable doing it. After a while I noticed that they slowly avoided me. Guess they must have had too much of me. In addition, I felt that my peers were not impressed with my team. They were not cooperative and as such it was really hard to get support and resources to get things done. I did not have a great relationship with my peers either in the very beginning. I believe that my team recognized that. As a result, my department

struggled to get support and resources. Those were some of my worst moments in my managerial career."

The first time managers continue to operate still in their own comfort zones during this stage. They want to prove themselves. Hence, the best way is to leverage on their current strengths to add value to their subordinates. Somewhere down the line, Johan, for example ended up following his subordinates to see clients and be involved in their planning sessions. This is not exactly what his subordinates wanted which explains why they avoided him after a while.

On the flip side, the subordinates typically are still very sceptical of their new managers. They are not sure where their managers come from. They doubt their managers' interests. Unless the managers demonstrate genuine interests in their subordinates, it will be very hard for the new managers to gain support.

These situations will go on for months. New managers find themselves entangled in the web of solving problems, resolving conflicts, negotiating to secure resources and making decisions. Everyday proves to be the same. Slowly, they start to realize that their perception of having the formal authority is not exactly the way they have visualized it.

After a while, they start to hear feedback on their performances both directly and indirectly. In Johan's example, he recognizes some of the feedback that he receives in his third and fourth month in the role as depicted below:

> "My manager is not showing me the big picture and the direction that we are heading. So far I do not see any added value from him."

> "My manager is not spending enough time with me. He seems to be spending a lot more time with my other peers, going with them to see clients and help them solve problems. I am not sure that he even cares about what I do."

"My manager has to know what he has to do. I brought him to my clients at his request and he ended up taking over the conversations the whole time even when I have already told him which part he has to get involved in. I am suffocated because he is doing my job."

"Your team just came to see me at the 11th hour asking for additional resources to help fix a situation for her clients . . . worse still, she expected to get the resources right away. And this was the fourth request that I received from your team today. Didn't she understand the process in this organization? I have so many other important requests from other more important customers that deserve those resources. Can you just guide them to do it the right way?"

"Johan, I am not impressed with your team. They are poor at planning. Everything they want is urgent. And oftentimes, their briefs on customer requirements are not accurate. It is hard working with your team."

"Johan, I have not received the detailed plan of your top three projects yet. And it has been three months since I asked for it. I cannot provide the right resources and support without a concrete plan. You seem to be going all over the place. It is time to step up your planning and organizing skills to get any help from us."

"Johan, I haven't seen you for a while now. You must have been real busy. How are you getting along with your people and your peers? What are your priorities this year?"

Hearing the above feedback makes Johan realized that his initial perception of what the managerial role is all about was totally wrong. All of a sudden he knows that he has failed in getting his team members to follow his instructions. In addition, he feels helpless as he is tired of doing everything without much help from others. He starts to ponder on the potential reasons as to why it is very hard for him to take control of his department. The questions from his direct manager at this juncture make him very nervous: Firstly, because he has not made efforts to see and update his direct manager ever since he takes up the role and secondly, because his direct manager specifically highlights on relationships with subordinates and peers. It indicates that something may have gone really wrong. The new manager is not sure what to do.

How do first time managers respond to such feedback? Evidently, some respond positively and some do not. Those who respond positively will receive the feedback in a constructive manner and revisit all their events and activities that have taken place since they become managers. They even ask for further feedback to understand where they go wrong.

In Johan's scenario, he makes a point to sit down with his direct manager, his team members and his peers. He conducts open conversations with them with the goal to improve on his performance. During his conversations with the respective stakeholders, he focuses on three key questions; what's working, what's not and what should be done differently? The key findings of the conversations are:

- Being too overwhelmed with operational issues daily, Johan does not have the time to do proper planning and to clearly set the direction for his department.
- Formal authority does not exist. Johan finally understands that he has to earn it. The title of a manager does not make him any different from anyone of his team members. He still needs to build credibility, earn trust and respect before he can discharge authority.
- Assuming that his team members will support him automatically just because he is their manager is wrong. They need to understand what is in it for them before they can extend undivided support to Johan.

- Building relationship with all his stakeholders is crucial as Johan is dependent on them to get things done. In this scenario, he knows that building relationship is crucial but he cannot believe that in his first few months he overlooks it completely due to the amount of issues that he has to deal with.

- Johan's peers do not respect his team because of his poor relationship with them and the haphazard approach of his team members when requesting for support and resources.

- The types of changes that the role of a manager brings about are daunting. Johan concludes that he does not manage the change as well as he possibly can. He has the tendency to operate in his own comfort zone which results in his skewed focus towards selected team members that he is more comfortable with.

- Johan does not take the time to get to know his team members really well. He applies the same approach to everyone which backfires after a while.

Based on the findings, Johan starts working on a renewed approach to managing which he shares with his direct manager to seek relevant feedback and ensure continuous monitoring.

Stage 3: Readjustment

The renewed approach that Johan adopted is:

- **Take the time to plan and set direction for his department:** With the help from his direct manager, Johan starts putting together the overall vision of the department in line with the organizational goals articulating where it is heading, where it is at now and identifying the gaps and the how-to execution plans to achieve the desired outcomes. The directions include financial, organizational and business. He establishes specific forms of communications to deliver this message. For example, he announces it during his team meeting, and then follows up officially with an email. During the team meeting, he asks for his team's feedback to further strengthen the planned direction. In addition, he encourages his team members to approach him anytime they need specific clarifications.

- **Proactively build relationship and set predictable rules of engagements with his direct manager and peers:** Johan deliberately establishes a mutually rewarding partnership with his direct manager by openly asking his preferred modus operandi. For instance, frequency of face time in a week and freedom in decision making. They mutually agree on the types of measures to be monitored and reported in a standard format on a weekly basis. Johan's key objective is to have full understanding on what is expected of him in both the short and long term. With his peers, Johan starts to build a network with them. He has informal chats to understand his peers' priorities and goals. He deliberately discusses on how to be successful together as a team in line with the organizational goals. The outcomes of such conversations are they agree to reset their relationships anew by treating each other with respect. They manage to formulate on how their respective departments shall, can and will work together. They gradually come up with their mutual "service level agreement" that will be treated as the work blueprint between their respective departments. In addition, they formulate shared goals among departments which will be measured throughout the year. Johan and his peers create joint-communication messages on the agreed work blueprint to be communicated to their respective employees.

- **Communicate inter department's rule of working together:** Johan communicates to his team members on the urgent need to change their behaviours in order to shift the unfavourable perception that they have suffered as a department. He conducts interactive feedback session with all his team members discussing on the types of improvements that they need to undertake. He singles out the need to plan and organize effectively especially when it comes to requesting for support and resources. He follows up on the joint communication messages and coaches his team members on how to utilize the work blueprint. He starts prioritizing current projects, future projects, mapping out activities and resources required. To ensure compliance, they agree to monitor progress of project priorities on a weekly basis. In addition, they agree to include their peers in the loop of the project progress on a regular basis as well.

- **Personalized engagement with his team members:** Johan takes the time to understand the various needs of his team members. He now recognizes that his team members consist of four unique categories:

  o **The Stars:** The star performers and experienced personnel want the freedom to be on their own, to exercise their creativity with the least amount of intervention from their manager. For this group, Johan starts to shift his focus to sharing more of high level strategy discussion, seeking feedback in setting direction for the department and helping them in situations only when they require him to do so. In addition, Johan gives them the opportunity to stretch their capabilities to develop their career further. For instance, Johan assigns them to mentor the new hires and selects them to be the change agents for the team. A star employee who is excellent in his approach to selling solutions and engaging high level decision makers is assigned to share his best practices to the rest of the team members and to coach other team members to replicate such approach.

  o **The Average Performers:** This group feels neglected and that Johan is not interested in their success. Johan decides to introduce recurring 1:1 meeting and officially announces his open door policy. The 1:1 meeting provides the platform for them to talk about anything that they wish to talk about (including personal matters). His subordinates set the agenda and Johan is expected to listen and respond accordingly. The open door policy sets the tone that the manager is available at any time for the subordinates to engage with on any issues. Johan starts to coach his subordinates on the specific issues as required, using the same opportunity to challenge them to step up their performances. As a result, his subordinates feel appreciated as Johan is always providing guidance and leads them to find answers for themselves, rather than telling or directing them on what he feels is right.

o **The New Employees:** This group receives the most attention from Johan in the first five months because he assumes that the new employees need more guidance. Also, he is most comfortable with them. Johan wants to add value so much to the subordinates that he helps the new employees in almost everything that he is comfortable doing, or the areas that he is so successful at when he was an individual contributor. Thereafter, he changes his approach to provide less hand holding. He provides them more space to breathe and function on their own. The modus operandi then moves to coaching, proactively planning with the new employees by asking them the right questions for them to come up with their own answers and solutions. Johan follows up on their progresses constantly to ensure that they are assimilating well within the organization.

o **The Challenged Employees:** Two major reasons that employees fall within this group are failure to perform to expectations and mismatched of skill sets to roles. Johan asks for advice on how to approach this group from both his direct manager and the Human Resource Manager. As a result he initiates 1:1 conversations with them and conducts open discussions on what they feel about their overall performances. Johan then provides initial guidance and discusses on the immediate tasks and results that they need to accomplish, followed by weekly follow ups on the progress of the agreed tasks. Johan monitors the weekly progress with recommendations on how to improve performance on continuous basis. Within six months if they improve satisfactorily as planned, then they will stay on the job. If they do not, specific actions will be taken and managed in the best way possible. For failure to perform to expectations scenario, the outcome may be job termination. For mismatched of skill sets to role, the outcome may be taking a different role suitable to the employee in a different department.

- **Managing change:** Johan makes an effort to remind himself of the required transition from an individual contributor to people manager that he needs to self-manage. He approaches it in two ways:

  o **Doing the work of a manager:** Johan starts to be selective and focuses on how he uses his time. He allocates time for planning, developing and maintaining operations. As far as engagement with his team members is concerned, he shifts towards becoming a coach and mentor, giving more empowerment to them. He shifts towards providing the right and required skills, resources and knowledge for his team members to do their jobs rather than hand holding them over every step of the way to get things done, regardless of how comfortable he is with certain tasks. He also demonstrates his accountability to the team by not penalizing them when they make mistakes. This is illustrated when one of his subordinates, Emma, gives some discount that is not within her approval limit to her potential clients with the intention of informing him much later when she returns to the office. Unfortunately, Emma forgets about it. A week later, the Finance Manager, David, is after Emma when he tracks the order and finds that specific company policy is compromised. Emma is so taken aback by the whole event. She confides in Johan that she knows she has to ask for his approval and is confident that Johan would have approved it. Hence, she decides to bite the bullet and agrees with the client as she badly needs to secure the business. She wants to inform Johan about it as soon as she returns to the office but she totally forgets about it until the time that David comes around to look for her. To Emma's surprise, Johan is calm about it. He confirms that what Emma did was wrong and she should not repeat the same mistake again in the future. He advises Emma to just ring him up anytime that she needs such approval in the future. He stresses that he should be consulted for any discount considerations. He then informs Emma that he will take the ownership and explains to David about the whole situation. Emma is so relieved. Johan impresses her a great deal in demonstrating that his interest is genuinely for the department and the organization, and not for himself. Emma feels that she can really trust Johan as a manager from then on.

o **Inject as much predictability as possible into his operations:** Johan introduces structured processes of engagement to avoid randomizing his teams' works in the field. He establishes a well structured monthly department meeting, fortnightly 30 minute session of 1:1 meetings with each of his team member and enforces his open door policy ensuring his availability whenever they need him.

o **Enhance teamwork by introducing informal team activities:** Johan starts getting his team members together for informal activities such as going to the movies once a month, celebrating birthdays for his team members and getting involved in some community work related to their industry. In addition, at times, he invites his peers and their respective team members as well. This gives the opportunity for everyone to bond with each other which benefits them immensely at work. They understand each other better and will go the extra mile to help each other succeed.

o **Stay healthy to manage stress better:** The managerial role can be very stressful at times. Learning from the first five months Johan includes time to exercise three times a week to recharge his energy. He finds this to be very effective as not only does it make him very alert in his work, it also makes him very disciplined and focused, which in turn enhances his productivity.

Stage 4: Coming Together

The readjustment stage brings about many changes to Johan and his team. There is more predictability in his department and his subordinates gradually get used to the way their department functions. All of a sudden, there is a rhythm being established which everyone starts to adhere to.

Johan feels that as well. However, he is not sure how he can leverage such situation until a significant event takes place as described below:

> Johan has a weekly sales meeting which is mandatory for all of his team members to attend. One of his star performers, Jeff, does not attend the sales meeting for three weeks in a row. It is not a big issue to Johan as Jeff updates him on his accounts regularly. Besides, it is not much of his concern as Jeff hardly fails to deliver on his commitments. Hence, he does not take any actions on Jeff as he would have on others. A few weeks later, his Human Resource Manager, Amir, drops by his office and informs Johan that a few of his team members has expressed dissatisfaction of his favouritism practice. They demand consistent practices for everyone in the whole department. Johan is surprised to hear such accusations. He feels that he is misunderstood. However, he takes action to remedy that by asking for an apology from his team members and agrees on what he will be doing differently in the future.

Johan learns from the above event that his actions or decisions on one subordinate will impact the rest of the team members. He recognizes that he holds a certain power and can influence the group's behaviour towards a certain direction. This is exactly what he has been feeling after he readjusted his overall approach to the group. He then understands that he has the power to orchestrate people for a common purpose by establishing a certain context or creating a specific environment for them.

This is the time when Johan is ready to establish the departmental culture and its strategic vision for the long term. His team members respect and trust him. They are ready to follow and support him. Johan has stepped up his role to the next level, managing his team members as a group rather than managing each individually.

Perspective 2: Operating Environment

Upon understanding the four stages that new managers typically go through, let us take a look at the kind of operating environment that new managers operate in. What are the common characteristics of their operating environment?

The real life experiences of the first time managers in the first twelve months indicate these characteristics:

- **Ambiguous**: New managers operate in a fluid environment with much uncertainty. It is common for them to feel pulled towards multiple directions haphazardly.
- **Multiple and varied demands from many stakeholders at the same time**: Everyone seems to want a piece of the new manager; the subordinates, the peers, the direct manager as well as external contacts such as customers and business partners. And each one of them has different expectations of the new manager.
- **Formal authority yet very dependent**: The title of a manager is mistakenly assumed by many new managers as formal authority that entitles them to get support and followers from day one on

the job. In contrast, new manager has to invest time building relationship and proving to his team that their interests come first before he can earn trust and respect from his team members.

- **Balancing tradeoffs**: Oftentimes organizational needs are in conflict with people's and customer's needs. New managers need to learn the art of balancing the respective trade-offs.

- **Listen well**: The ability to listen well is absolutely necessary. New managers are faced with issues everyday that affect many people across the board and they are expected to solve problems and make informed decisions in a timely manner. Listening well helps in focusing on the right issues and works on solving problems effectively.

- **Good working relationship is a must**: New managers will not succeed unless they manage to build good working relationship with their subordinates, their peers, direct managers, customers, business partners and other stakeholders. This is critical as they depend on people to achieve their desired results. They have to be able to orchestrate teams and the relevant stakeholders to work together for a common purpose.

- **Required to make decision without enough information:** One of the key roles of managers is to make informed and timely decision. In the real world, so many things happen at the same time with differing variables that it is hard for the managers to have all the information available simultaneously. Hence there will be circumstances that call for some degree of judgment and intuition from the managers. In such scenarios, they have to know how to make the best decision on time even when there is not enough information made available to them.

Perspective 3: Key Challenges

The four evolutionary stages (Honeymoon, Reality, Readjustment and Coming Together) of the real life experiences of new managers depict these key challenges faced by new managers:

- **Setting direction for their departments:** Managers need to have the capability to see the big picture, a deep understanding of the business that their respective organizations are in and how best their departments can contribute to the overall success of the organization. While a lot is expected from a Sales Director in growing business for the organization; the same should be expected from a Human Resource Director in terms of providing the right support, learning and development plan for other departments in the organization. As such, every manager shall establish his respective departmental directions to mutually complement each other so as to support the common organizational vision. While many new managers may plan to set a time to establish this at the onset; they fall short of achieving it as demands of the daily operational issues easily take over. Coupled with their lack of readiness to manage change in their new role, they will continue operating in their own comfort zones and will end up "fire fighting" on regular basis.

- **Managing tradeoffs:** Can a manager satisfy every one of his stakeholders at any one time? Oftentimes, the answer is no. It is quite common that the organization's needs contradict with the team members' or customers' needs. For example, a US-based multinational corporation which is about to sign a contract with a customer in Malaysia makes it mandatory that the contract must be based on the US law. However, the customer requests that such clause be amended to the Malaysian law. A manager obviously will find himself in a sticky situation as the outcome may well be that the contract will not be signed. Situations like this call for the manager to exercise his best effort to achieve the most optimized results that will benefit his organization first.

- **Connecting with people effectively:** A manager needs good interpersonal skills to be successful. Being dependent on the subordinates to achieve his desired results, he must be able to secure their commitments to execute on the required tasks and effectively manage their performances. So, how does a manager secure their subordinates' commitments? The simple answer is one has to invest time to establish credibility with the subordinates. Credibility comes with trust and respect. One of the best ways to earn trust and respect is to demonstrate that their interests come first. The story about Johan not penalizing Emma for making a mistake and taking full responsibility of it as described earlier is a good example of this. Johan demonstrates that he is there for Emma and cares about her success. Other considerations to secure the team's commitment include creating a two way feedback ready environment in an open and respectful manner (manager to subordinates and subordinates to manager). Managers have to be mentally ready to take criticism and challenges from their subordinates. Avoid being defensive. Subordinates will appreciate their willingness to listen and the opportunity for them to express their opinions. Over time, they will begin to respect and trust their managers. In addition, managers can also opt for a participative management style by getting subordinates involved in some of the decision making processes, seeking their views before a decision is made, explaining the reasons why certain things are done in favour of the other and calling for new ideas for specific initiatives. The moment they are involved and their ideas are implemented, they will be committed as they are a part of the "creators" of the ideas or initiatives in the first place.

- **Sustaining subordinates' commitment:** What's next once a manager succeeds in securing his team's commitment? Moving on is about sustaining their commitment. How can one ensure that their commitment is constantly at the highest level? It has to do a lot with motivation. While money may be one method of motivation, subordinates do appreciate other methods of motivation as well. Beyond money, one has the option to institute other incentives such as periodic initiative-based incentive or ad-hoc initiative. An example of the periodic initiative-based incentive is quarterly winner of forecast accuracy within $\pm 5\%$.

An ad-hoc incentive is meant to demonstrate appreciation for efforts done more than the expected scope of duty.

- **Leading the team:** When will a manager be able to successfully lead the team? A manager will be successful at this when his team members are ready to be led or they are fully committed (a manager has earned their respect and trust and they believe he has their interests at heart) to his cause. It is critical for a manager to establish consistent practices and procedures for his team members to adhere to. Compliance is a necessity applicable to everyone. One of the most challenging areas in leading the team is managing individual subordinate's performance. One cannot apply a "one size fits all" approach. The four unique categories require distinctive approaches as described below:

    o **The Star Performers:** Very experienced and excellent performers. Their expectations are for the managers to give them the right attention and a lot of freedom for them to do their work as they function best when they are independent. They value the manager's contribution in providing them the big picture, giving them the sense of direction and goals of the organization, recognizing their accomplishments and investing in their future career development.

    o **The Average Performers:** Tend to feel neglected and unsure of the manager's interest in their success because new manager tends to focus a lot of attention to the newer employees. The average performers do want some attention from their managers. They expect the managers to be approachable and readily available when needs be. Most importantly, they need the manager to coach and guide them in very specific areas, ranging from technical to business and commercial areas. And at times, they just need to engage with the managers to bounce off ideas.

    o **The New Employees:** New managers are very comfortable and confident at engaging with the new employees. As a result, they tend to get the most attention. The managers assume that they need a lot of hand holding in executing their tasks. Consequently, the managers may end up over managing them. Ideally, the new employees expect a certain degree of hand holding only in the beginning. Once they are familiar with the environment and the new culture that they operate in, they will only need specific coaching and guidance. They will end up feeling suffocated if the managers keep on their hand holding approach longer than required. As a result, they may end up avoiding the managers in the long run.

o **The Challenged Employees:** This group poses a pressing challenge to the new managers as they need to be able to effectively diagnose specific performance problem, provide the relevant feedback and make the hard decision whether to implement performance improvement programs or to remove them. In a way, this can be an emotional situation for the managers which they need to contain with. Constant communication is necessary to manage challenged employees. Discuss performance issues at the very early stages rather than delaying them. Having a regular checkpoint such as the 1:1 meeting will help a great deal as performance issues can be discussed and dealt with gradually. The employees will have the chance to discuss and provide feedback about their performances on a regular basis. They are aware of where they stand and will be able to have realistic expectations on the consequences of no improvement. The constant discussion and feedback will generate mutually agreed actions items on short term periodic improvement that both parties can work on. In the event that things do not work out in the end, the situation will be so much easier to manage as the employees are fully aware of where they stand all throughout the process.

- **Giving and receiving feedback effectively:** The purpose of feedback is to reinforce good behaviour and to rectify bad behaviour. It is important for new managers to handle the process of giving and receiving feedback effectively. It starts with the managers establishing a "feedback-ready" environment by demonstrating that they are open to receiving feedback and to taking specific actions as required. Unless the appropriate actions are taken, the subordinates will not trust that their feedback will make any difference. As a result, they will shy away from engaging in any feedback sessions. Key is for new managers to coach their subordinates on how to give and receive feedback respectfully. To kick it off, specific programs can be introduced to inculcate the culture of giving and receiving feedback.

A thorough understanding of the scope of being a manager, the environment that managers operate in and the key challenges will equip new managers with the right expectations of the managerial role. New managers can start preparing themselves by, first and foremost, adopting a mindset that they have to earn trust and respect from their subordinates and stakeholders alike. Then, they can start focusing on setting directions for their departments, building relationships with subordinates and stakeholders, getting to know their team members, deciding on the unique engagement style and encouraging open communications.

Action Items for New Managers

Consider focusing on three key priorities as listed below in your first thirty (30) days as a manager:

- **Set and communicate the direction for your department:**

  o Formulate a direction for your department in alignment with your organizational goals.

o   Have a dialogue with your team members and seek their feedback on the direction formulated.

o   Discuss with your superior and seek his/her feedback on the direction that you have formulated with your team members.

o   Communicate the final direction to your team members effectively.

• **Build relationships with your subordinates, superiors and peers:**

o   Deliberately establish a targeted plan in building relationships with your subordinates, superior and peers.

o   Have a customized approach with every one of them as you see applicable.

o   Discuss on the best way of working together.

• **Assess where your department stands currently and what is needed to achieve your goals:**

o   Take stocks of your current strengths, weaknesses, opportunities and threats.

o   Based on the direction you formulate initially, evaluate on the capabilities required to achieve your goals.

o   Identify gaps in capabilities.

o   Plan and budget to secure the identified capabilities.

CORNERSTONE 2: FUNCTION OF LEADERSHIP AND MANAGEMENT

Nᴇᴡ ᴍᴀɴᴀɢᴇʀs ɴᴇᴇᴅ ᴛᴏ ᴜɴᴅᴇʀsᴛᴀɴᴅ both leadership and management in order to have a good appreciation of their managerial role. Are leadership and management the same thing? Or are they different?

Two famous quotes below best described the function of leadership and management:

> "Management is doing things right and leadership is doing the right things." *Peter F Drucker.*

> "Leadership is about coping with change and management is about coping with complexity." *John P Kotter.*

Organizations operate in a highly interconnecting web of environment that poses complex and conflicting challenges. Externally, organizations need to address business challenges ranging from competitive threats, policy and regulatory changes, natural disasters affecting business, demographic trends such as aging population, economic situations and many others. Internally, organizations evolve through their own lifecycles from start-up, growth, maturity and consolidation. Each cycle presents its own challenges in terms of finance, personnel, systems and processes.

The combination of external and internal challenges place organizations in a state of uncertainty which is constantly changing. To survive and stay relevant, organizations must be agile, has the capability to change with the market dynamics, speedily and constantly thrive in addressing the complexity of the business.

For example, in the 1990s, Microsoft, the then number one software company in the world for two decades with its flagship platform Windows, found themselves in a challenging situation to further expand their revenue to the enterprise market segment. While their track record in providing great products to the small and mid market segments was excellent, the enterprise segment was not convinced that Microsoft had a robust and scalable platform to support the needs of the enterprise. They perceived Microsoft as not reliably proven in the enterprise and did not understand their business needs. Microsoft responded by embarking on a major initiative to transform its sales culture from "transactional selling" ("product centric") to "solution selling" ("customer centric").

The Vice President of Worldwide Enterprise Sales launched the transformational initiative, the Integrated Solution Selling (ISS), articulating the purpose of the transformation, its benefits and the opportunity cost of not adopting the ISS. He went into great details explaining the overall impact of the ISS and stated the urgent need for the Enterprise Division of Microsoft to adopt the new sales culture in order to stay relevant. The direction was crystal clear. All enterprise sales engagements from that moment would utilize and play by the ISS rules.

The ISS launching at the World Wide Sales and Marketing Managers Meeting (WWSMM) was further communicated to all employees in the Enterprise Division in every Microsoft subsidiary. They received his speech by email and listened to it on CDs. Videotape copies were also made available. In addition, every Enterprise Division leader in every subsidiary communicated with their team members and mapped out all action items needed for their implementation at the local level.

The directive to adopt the ISS sales culture resulted in a few strategic initiatives that include the establishment of Microsoft Solution Selling Process (MSSP), the implementation of Siebel Client Relationship Management (CRM) system, the creation of new roles in enterprise sales, the development of MSSP learning curriculum, the adoption of new role-based performance measures and a refined compensation plans to cater for the new changes in scopes and roles.

Evidently, Microsoft decision to adopt the ISS sales culture then, had ensured their relevance in the enterprise market segment until today. The transformation from "transactional selling" to "solution selling" was a success due to the tight synergy between the function of leadership and management.

The activities and tasks that demonstrated the function of **leadership** include the articulation of the transformational vision, communicating the vision to every level of the organization, aligning people towards the ISS culture, motivating and inspiring the employees to change by ensuring that the changes would be as painless and bring huge benefits to them.

The activities and tasks that demonstrated the function of **management** include the establishment of the MSSP, the implementation of the Siebel CRM, the creation of new roles in enterprise sales, the development of the MSSP learning curriculum, the adoption of new role-based performance measures and a refined compensation plans to cater for the new changes in scopes and roles.

Leadership is about being visionary in setting direction of the organization, aligning people, motivating and inspiring others to embrace change[1]. Management is about making things happen, translating vision into reality, getting the team members to execute and perform within the respective budget and environment provided for them. The key activities within management are plan and budget, organize and staff and control and solve problem[2].

Three Big Ideas on Leadership

Let us explore three big ideas on leadership to gain further insights on its function.

Idea 1:
Everyone is a leader, hence leadership starts with you

Diagram 2 depicts the traditional mindset in many organizations that you have to be at a certain managerial position, with specific titles for you to be a leader. Unless you are in such a pedestal, you are merely a follower.

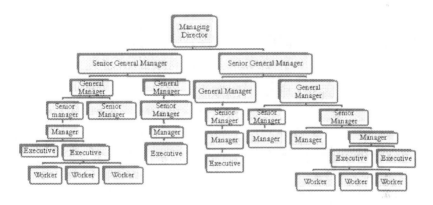

Diagram 2: Typical Hierarchy of Organization

Let us break the traditional mindset. Leadership starts with you as you have the power to choose the path that you aspire. You do not need a title to practice leadership. For example, even if you are currently an individual contributor at the very bottom of the hierarchy of your organization, you are very much responsible and accountable for the direction that you want to take in leading your work and your life. The kind of questions that you will be asking yourself is very similar to the kind of questions that organizations will use in establishing their directions. For example, "where are we now?", "where are we going?", "what are our strengths and weaknesses?", "how do we get to where we want to go?", "what has worked well?", "what hasn't worked well?", "what should be done differently moving forward?". The answers to all these questions may help you in the following:

- To establish a specific direction towards achieving excellent results.
- To have a specific approach in managing the required changes to achieve the desired results.
- To have clear plans to align yourself with the environment that you are in.
- To be able to come up with periodic self-monitoring and reward schemes in order to continuously assess where you stand and motivate yourself for better results.

The basic principle is, regardless of the designated titles, every employee in any organization is a leader and a worker. While hierarchically organizations are structured in a typical pyramid as depicted in Diagram 2, everyone is expected to execute certain tasks and is compensated based on their capability to produce the expected results.

A Procurement Manager's task for instance, may be reducing procurement cost by 5% across the board and compensation is based on the collective results achieved by his team members. One of his direct reports, a Procurement Executive's task may be to ensure prompt payment to suppliers within 30 days. Accordingly, the Procurement Executive compensation is based on his direct contribution to achieve such result.

In this regard, the manager is as much a worker as his subordinate. And the subordinate is as much a leader as his direct manager. Both are responsible and accountable to their respective functions. And both are answerable to someone. Even a CEO is answerable to the Board of Directors. Each one of them has to have personal leadership: having the vision on how to execute tasks effectively, aligning and supporting the organizational goals and strong interest and motivation to get the job done well. The stronger the personal leadership one has, the more efficient one will be in producing results.

Another key aspect in organizations today is a strong dependency among team members from multiple departments to achieve certain results. An IT sales team requires the assistance from developers, solution architects and process consultants in delivering solutions to their clients. Such cross group collaboration requires strong leadership skills such as persuasive communications, managing conflicts, dealing with ambiguity, managing time effectively and many others. Getting the intended outcomes call for the team members to practice leadership skills fitting to specific situations regardless of their titles and positions.

In conclusion, everyone is a leader regardless of titles and positions in the organizational hierarchy. Organizations stand to benefit a great deal if their employees choose to practice personal leadership at all times.

Idea 2:
Great leaders bring the best out of their people

Sir Alex Ferguson, the Manager of Manchester United Football Club has won 48 trophies to-date, making him the most successful British football manager in history[3].

Since managing Manchester United in 1986, he has managed to achieve very consistent performance for the Club despite the fact that players come and go and setbacks in terms of fitness and injuries did occur in every football season.

Carlo Ancelloti, the former manager of Chelsea Football Club in fact recognized Ferguson's leadership capabilities, as quoted in The Daily Mirror, "As a coach, he is unusual. It's not as if he guides the training sessions because he delegates a lot and has an excellent staff. But he understands football like few do. With him, all the players improve. He has no fear of introducing youngsters."[4] Ancelloti concurred that Ferguson has a way with his people, knowing exactly how to inspire and motivate them to pursue specific results.

He knows how to delegate effectively. He places undivided trust in all his players, experienced as well as inexperienced young players. He brings out the best in them. Time and time again, Ferguson appears to be doing the right things at just the right time, and inevitably Manchester United ends up being the Champion.

How can you be like Sir Alex Ferguson in your management setting? You can bring out the best in your people by adopting these approaches:

- **Trust them**: You have to demonstrate that you trust them. You believe in their capabilities to produce great results and give them freedom to execute their innovative and creative ideas.
- **Focus on their strengths**: Your team members have their own strengths and weaknesses. Key is for you to focus on their strengths and encourage them to realize their full potential.
- **Promote continuous improvement**: You need to create an ongoing learning culture for continuous improvement. Encourage them to share their key learning with the team members. Create a common platform to ease the knowledge sharing process such as your department's best practices intranet or a short sharing session for everyone during your staff meeting.
- **Encourage dialogue and debate for decision making**: Practice participative management style. Promote dialogue among team members. Brainstorm on approaches and issues to find resolution. This will result in a strong sense of ownership and accountability due to their involvement in the decision making process.
- **Celebrate success and give recognition when due**: Adopt reward for results approach. Celebrate success no matter how small. In fact, for long term project, divide it into small milestones and celebrate small successes once a milestone is achieved. Your team members will feel appreciated and motivated to sustain excellent performance continuously.
- **Keep on increasing the bar for high performance**: Keep on challenging your team members to realize their full potentials. Whenever they achieve their goals, suggest a higher and bigger goal. Let them voice their opinions about the challenges you suggest. Discuss reservations if they have any. Offer solutions to their reservations. Do not stop persuading until they agree to some stretched goals.

Idea 3:
Great leaders excel at connecting with people

Have you ever met people who make you feel at ease right away even when you are meeting them for the first time? You feel that they are extremely approachable, genuinely care about you and engagingly present. As a result, you are convinced and easily persuaded to undertake certain tasks or projects under their supervisions.

These individuals are excellent at connecting with people. They are extremely aware of their own strengths and weaknesses. They have a superb capability in managing their composure, positively reacting to situations around them. They build effective relationships because they are able to sense the perspectives and feelings of others, taking active interest in their concerns. They are also very skilful in providing guidance, able to take charge and can be very persuasive when needs be. They are high achievers. They will always search for the best because they are very passionate in what they do.

These are the traits of great leaders. They have high emotional intelligence which comprises of these competencies: self awareness, self management, social awareness and social skills.[5]

Likewise, you can connect with people effectively by adopting these approaches:

- **Being aware of your own strengths and weaknesses**: Know your strengths and always be honest of your own capabilities. You are not expected to know everything. Create self-deprecating sense of humour when you talk about such subject. You have to feel comfortable admitting that maybe your team members are smarter than you in some areas. Make full use of that. Empower them to own and be accountable in the areas that you think they will excel in.
- **Listening well**: Practice active listening. Your team members will value your wholehearted engagement with them. It drives the

message that you think they are important and you value their opinions.

- **Exercising empathy**: Imagine yourself in their shoes. Try to understand their situation as best as you can, along with other factors when making decisions.
- **Having motivation**: Be a passionate manager. You are driven to achieve beyond expectations simply because you are so passionate for the work itself. Raise the bar continuously and keep score of your performance.
- **Being reasonable**: Create an environment of trust and fairness. You must be able to control your feelings and impulses. Take the time to understand the relevant situations with an open mind. Make a smart choice and take appropriate actions once you have considered all the options.
- **Being persuasive in a friendly manner**: Make yourself approachable and friendly. Focus on common grounds in building relationship. Offer help and pay attention to your team members' concerns. Convince them on the benefits of specific actions that you want them to execute. Ensure that they fully understand the kind of impact and differences that their contributions will make to the organization.

Three Big Ideas on Management

Let us now explore three big ideas on management to gain further insights on its function:

Idea 1:
Great managers are very effective at setting direction and building relationship

The thrust of a manager delivers results through people in line with the organizational goals.

Great managers are aware from the onset that their success depends on the following:

- The willingness of their subordinates to cooperate and work together among each other in executing their tasks.
- Capable and smart people working for them. As such, they do not view capable and smart people as a threat to them.
- Their effectiveness in providing the right support and infrastructure for their subordinates to function at the most optimum level.

In this case, great managers realize that their role is to orchestrate, serve and provide their team members with the best conducive environment for them to perform. They prioritize on setting direction and building relationship as the two most important factors to them.

The key in achieving this is the managers' ability to set and communicate effectively the direction of the organization as well as their respective departments, how to get there and what's expected from every team member at any one point in time. In addition, they establish specific strategy in building relationships with both internal (subordinates, direct managers and peers) and external (customers, business partners, government and community leaders) networks.

Idea 2:
Great managers earn trust and respect from team members over time to properly discharge authorities

Authority is neither an entitlement nor automatic. It has to be earned. It comes with credibility.

Great managers establish credibility by earning trust and respect from their subordinates. They invest time in engaging the subordinates, offering the right touch, coaching and guiding as appropriate and listening actively when the subordinates discuss about issues, not limiting to just work. They keep a very open approach, lending their ears as they have genuine interest in their well beings.

They take ownership of difficult situations that their subordinates may experience. Great managers are supportive when their subordinates make unintentional mistakes. They help find resolution and have a constructive feedback session with them, taking stock of what happen, discussing on what's working and what's not. Moving forward, they follow up with what will be done differently. Subordinates have the safety net and learn from their mistakes. They know that their managers care about them and have their interests at heart. This will result in them respecting and trusting their managers.

Over time the trust and respect established will grow into solid commitment from the subordinates. When there is trust and respect, it is easy for both parties to communicate effectively. Managers feel comfortable to manage in a participatory manner, seeking feedback from the subordinates on specific ideas and constructively discussing ways to approach certain issues and find resolutions. Managers become proactive in communicating on why things are done in a certain way. The subordinates end up feeling that they can count on the managers and completely buy in to their purposes. The strong commitments and buy-ins from the subordinates enable managers to discharge their authorities completely.

Idea 3:
Great managers provide performance feedback to their subordinates consistently and in a timely manner

Great managers do not wait until it is too late. They are hard core about consistently giving feedback to their subordinates on how they are doing, where they stand and discuss proactively on how to improve. They provide precise feedback articulating their observations on specific situations and incidents without biased personal attacks on the subordinates.

The key guidance on engagement is not about the "blame game" rather about taking stocks of events, incidents and agreement on three key aspects: what's working, what's not and what should be done differently.

When giving feedback, timing is of an essence. Great managers provide feedback of an event or incident promptly. This demonstrates genuine interest for continuous improvement. Communicating feedback late may send the wrong message to the subordinates. They may misconstrue it as their being picked on and the managers are not sincere about wanting them to improve.

In a nutshell, when giving feedback, consider the following:

- Focus on the performance action or result, not the person. Never accuse the employee.
- Provide feedback on a timely basis, but not too immediate if any party has strong emotions lingering.
- Provide coaching guidance, but also seek feedback on said guidance.
- Close the feedback session with the salient learning points, so that your subordinates grow from the experience.

And when receiving feedback, consider the following:

- Focus on the main objective of feedback which is to reinforce or rectify behaviour. Do not take it personally.
- Listen well and ask questions when you need clarifications.
- Assume good intentions from the person giving feedback.
- Ask what needs to be done differently.
- Thank the person giving you feedback, summarize your learning points and execute the agreed action items.

Conclusion

Leadership and management complement each other[6]. Managers have to practice both. They must be able to bring people on board to achieve a common purpose. They must also be able to plan, budget, organize, staff, control and solve problem within their own constrains and environment. They need to do this effectively.

So, what is the right mix? How much leadership and management should a manager apply at any one time? There may not be a straight forward answer to this. However, managers have to know that they need to apply both to suit their own environment appropriately. Each environment is unique.

Action Items for New Managers

Consider the following scenarios, plan on how you will address such situations and execute your plans effectively:

- **Scenario 1:** Observe your current team members. Identify those whom you feel are not practicing personal leadership. Understand why they are not practicing it. Think of ways to encourage them to practice personal leadership. Set a time, have one-on-one dialogue with each one of them and agree on specific actions moving forward.

- **Scenario 2:** Rate yourself in your effectiveness to connect with people. On a scale of between 1 (poor) and 5 (excellent), where do you stand? Think of improvement areas that you would like to pursue. Develop a short term plan to improve. Execute the plan. Repeat the same process till you rate yourself at your desired level.

- **Scenario 3:** Think of the most recent feedback sessions that you had with your subordinates. What happened during the sessions? Capture what's working and what's not. Decide on what you want to do differently in the next feedback sessions. Execute in your next feedback sessions. Repeat the same process until you master the skills of giving and receiving feedback.

CORNERSTONE 3:
BEHAVIOURAL SKILLS

Behavioural skills in this context refer to the types of skills needed for managers to be successful in their roles.

The core behavioural skills are:

- Setting direction
- Helping employees succeed
- Managing time and priorities
- Delegation
- Teamwork
- Planning and organizing
- Communication
- Problem solving
- Managing performance

Setting Direction

Setting direction has to be done right from the beginning as this will steer the direction of the department in line with the organizational goals. Invest time in doing this and seek feedback from your direct managers, peers and mentors in developing the agenda of the department.

You need to work on three variables to set direction effectively:

- **Clarity on direction and its purpose:** This is about articulating the direction, the purpose of adopting such direction and the benefits of heading to such destination. All that needs to be explained basically address the questions of where, what, why, how, when, who and how much.
- **Secure buy-in at the onset:** Once a direction has been set, you need to create a value proposition targeted for the varied audiences. This then, has to be socialized, reaching out to all the respective audiences, demonstrating the benefits of your direction to them.
- **Address resistance:** Additional outreach programs need to be established for the non-receptive audiences. Understand their resistances and develop additional programs to further communicate the benefits and address their resistances.

Helping Employees Succeed

Managers help their stakeholders succeed in order to be successful. Hence, it is critical that managers understand and appreciate the diverse needs of their stakeholders, comprising of their subordinates (Experienced, Average, New, and Challenged), peers and direct managers. Every stakeholder expects differently and managers need to be sensitive towards them and respond appropriately. For example, with peers, managers may spend a great deal of time building relationship and negotiating on resources while with direct managers, they discuss company strategy, plans for the business units and people development.

Many organizations today create a predictive operating environment that drives specific behaviour from their employees in their pursuit to holistically help them succeed. The predictive operating environment can be established by having a systemic pulse of operations. One of the best practices of systemic pulse of operations is the Microsoft Rhythm of Business (ROB).

The ROB is a structured, recurring schedule of critical meetings, activities and events that have very high impact to the overall business and operations.

The main objectives of establishing the ROB are to inject a certain degree of predictability to the business and secure commitment from key business leaders of their participations at the onset. The rules of engagement for the ROB are the committed schedule of activities is fixed and those involved are expected to be present at the stipulated date and time while mode of meetings can be in person, teleconference, video conference or by phone.

Prior to each meeting, the relevant participants fill in the meeting templates and upload them to a central shared folder. All meeting participants are authorized to have access to the shared folder. During meetings, participants are able to access all the documents and walk through the details as required.

There are multiple levels of ROB unique to the organization and business operations. Below is the example of an ROB for a local Microsoft subsidiary:

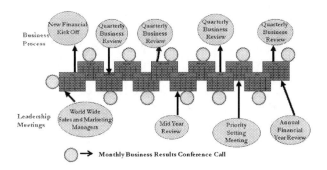

Diagram 3: Systemic Pulse of Operations Example

While the systemic pulse of operations set the operational rhythm for the business to function, the respective stakeholders will deliver the results expected of them when they:

- Fully understand and recognize what the expected results are and more importantly, their direct contributions for those results.
- Have crystal clear understanding of their scope of work and what success really means from the manager's point of view.
- Have a healthy engagement on mutual expectations.
- Proactively discuss and reach mutual agreement on the key measures for the desired results.
- Are ready to update progress on a timely basis and follow up on action items as scheduled.
- Accept and agree that the checkpoint progress is about continuous improvement.
- Have an open operating environment based on high quality standards and excellence as well as safe to make mistakes without getting penalized. Everyone learns from making mistakes.
- Trust that the spirit of communicating bad news is about constructively finding solutions to a real problem for a much bigger purpose, the well being of the organization.
- Believe in constructive intervention, understand that help is always around when needed and all they need to do is ask and that is expected of them.
- Function in an environment that celebrates success, big and small.
- Practice continuous learning. Share the success stories for others to learn and apply when needed.
- Finish what they start or get the job done.
- Expect excellent execution anytime, every time at all times.

The ROB can be implemented in big as well as small organizations. It can be streamlined to small departmental operations using these approaches:

- Create your own departmental calendar.
- Lock in recurring dates for your key departmental meetings such as staff meeting, sales meeting or other relevant meetings.
- Create a standard agenda and meeting templates (include instructions on how to use the template) for your meeting participants.
- Decide on methods to submit meeting templates. For example, whether to upload to a shared folder or to email meeting templates prior to the meeting.
- Commit your time as required.

Managing Time and Priorities

Time management is very critical for managers because of the never ending demand from the various stakeholders for the managers' time. Key is to prioritize all initiatives, activities and to ensure focus is on the right areas. Unless this is done, you may end up spending most of your time just fire fighting without any serious results at the end of the day.

Three types of activities that managers have to invest time on are **planning, developing and maintaining**.

Planning is about looking ahead, establishing a definitive roadmap that the organization will be adhering to within a specific timeframe. Key activities include setting direction, creating long term vision, defining financial, business and organizational objectives, articulating strategic initiatives that need to be executed, highlighting challenges, roadblocks and showstoppers, detailing competitive strategy and approaches to win. Managers must be able to balance priorities and decide on the best course of action that will produce the greatest result and benefit to the organization.

Developing is about equipping organizations with the right capabilities, skills, knowledge as well as infrastructure. This involves investment in resources: capital, physical and human, to realize the stated vision and direction. Managers are also expected to collaboratively determine their subordinate's learning and development plan, proactively coach the subordinates on how to set performance goals and mutually agree on the appropriate performance measures. They need to invest in the right infrastructure to support all the required activities to realize their vision.

Maintaining is about operational excellence: securing optimal level of excellence in execution continuously. Managers have to be aware of how well their execution is at any given time and constantly work on continuous improvement to achieve the best level of performance.

Managers must ensure that their time is invested effectively among planning, developing and maintaining. One of the best methods to assess how you are spending your time is via Stephen Covey's time management model that works based on the four quadrants on the backdrop of level of importance and level of urgency[7]. The key guiding principle is effective management requires managers to invest more time in the *"important but not urgent activities"* such as preparation, crisis prevention, values clarification, planning and relationship building. If managers can adopt such practice, the organization would highly likely thrive on excellent execution which in turn, would result in less serious problems, unwanted crises and fire fighting.

Many managers, however, are prone to invest more time in the following types of activities:

- *"Important and urgent" activities:* these reflect very reactive modus operandi as managers tackle the issues as they arise and treat them all as equally important. Examples of activities include addressing crises, solving pressing problems, rushing to meet deadlines and fire fighting.
- *"Not important and urgent" activities:* these reflect poor planning or no planning at all. All decisions are based on time factor or perceived urgency rather than other intrinsic values critical to the organization. Examples of activities are being involved in many popular activities, responding to non-critical emails, posting on social media, talking with colleagues about the latest office rumour

in the corridor, responding to all phone calls indiscriminately and attending unscheduled meetings.

Delegation

Delegation is about empowerment. Managers empower their subordinates to perform or execute tasks in order to achieve the desired results within the stipulated policy and boundary of correct business practices. In this case, managers provide their subordinates the opportunity to stretch themselves, stepping up their skills a few notches in order to be effective.

Evidently, this means that managers need to be comfortable about placing trust and providing freedom for the subordinates to make their own decisions on specific situations. The prerequisite of effective delegation include the following:

- **Know your team well**: It is critical for the managers to have true knowledge about the capabilities, strengths and weaknesses of their team members. The basic elements that the managers need to know well about their team members are:

  o **Competence**: Level of competency of each team member in their jobs.

  o **Personal integrity**: One of the key responsibilities of the managers is to protect the organization's interests and maintain a reputable image based on its core values at all times. Hence, the integrity of subordinates is of paramount importance to ensure that they put the organization's interests above their personal interests in all the business dealings that they perform.

  o **Motivation**: Subordinates with high degree of motivation are self starters, get the job done and are able to sustain and persevere in challenging situations. Subordinates with low degree of motivation are not excited to make a difference in specific tasks and will easily give up in challenging situations.

- **Apply situational leadership and management**: At times when the subordinates need support, managers have to be able to cohesively be the sounding board. Listen well. Ask the right questions. Subordinates will be able to figure out the next course of actions by responding to the question asked, rather than receiving instructions from the managers.

- **Know what to delegate, how much and to whom**: In addition to knowing the subordinates well in terms of their levels of competency, personal integrity and motivation, managers also need to have their basic principles on deciding what, how much and whom to delegate. The basic principles of decision are unique to one's own environment. However, the guiding principles can be the following:

  o **What**: Define an additional scope of work as an extension to the current work with higher degree of complexity in decision making.

  o **How much**: Reach mutual agreement between manager and subordinate assessing the current situations and demands of the current work.

  o **Who**: Subordinates whom the manager feels are ready for the next challenge.

- **Know when to follow up and intervene**: Empowerment to subordinates does not mean that the managers are letting go fully. While subordinates have a great deal of freedom to make decisions and to call the shots, managers are still as accountable as the subordinates are on the outcomes. It is advisable that the managers do recurring checkpoints on the subordinates' progresses. This can be done either via physical meeting, video conferencing, phone calls or emails.

Teamwork

Teamwork is about having team members working together in an integrated manner to achieve a common purpose.

Managers need to deliberately promote teamwork among team members by:

- **Building relationship with these stakeholders:**

  o **Subordinates:** Managers need to invest time to get to know their subordinates well, listen actively in order to help solve problems and offer help when the subordinates make mistakes. Over time, they will earn respect, trust and credibility.

  o **Peers:** Peers are a big part of the overall support system of the managers. Managers need their help almost on a daily basis as every function in organizations is interrelated. Hence, it is critical for the managers to proactively build good relationship with their peers, establish common goals, develop shared goals and discuss collaborative initiatives on a regular basis. It is also necessary for managers and their peers to provide feedback to each other and exchange ideas to find resolutions to some pressing issues that they face at any given time.

  o **Direct managers:** A few important things that the managers need to establish at the onset with their direct managers:

    ▪ Firstly, managers have to seek advice from their direct managers on the best method of engagement between them. Direct managers may have their own preferences and styles. For example, one direct manager may prefer that managers update him via email on a weekly basis on status and only call him when necessary; and another direct manager may prefer that his managers have conversations with him three times a week, first thing in the morning on Monday, Wednesday and Friday. Whatever the preferences are, managers need to adapt to the mode that their direct managers are comfortable with. Managers need to agree on this, in the beginning, to set the right expectations and inject as much predictability as possible in their relationship with their managers.

- Secondly, the end goal that matters to the direct managers is results. However, results cannot be achieved unless managers are able to forge strong working relationship with all the stakeholders in the organization. Managers should consider sharing their direction very early on with all the stakeholders. In addition, agree on common goals, and establish customized operational level agreement which stipulates how teams will work together. Next is for managers to communicate the operational level agreement to the direct manager and agree on the best approach to monitor results on mutually agreed periodic basis.

- Thirdly, direct managers will appreciate timely status updates and typically hate surprises. Managers are expected to engage with the direct managers based on the agreed method of engagement for status updates and in the event that there were real surprises or bad news, managers are better off to proactively alert their direct managers about such event detailing what happened, why it happened and the course of actions that will be taken to remedy the situation. Be honest and open about the whole situation.

o **External parties such as customers and business partners:** Two key external stakeholders are customers and business partners. Organizations or businesses exist because of customers. Customers gain much added value because of business partners. For example, millions of customers possess iPhones which in turn, sustain Apple as a business concern. Customers download many third party applications from Apple's business partners that enable them to read digital books, access live score of the Barclays Premier League, play Scrabble and many others. Therefore, establishing good partnership with both customers and business partners are crucial. The underlying principle in establishing partnerships with them is to be hard core about customer service. Give the best service. Seek feedback continuously on customer service improvement. Engage with the customers' key leadership teams on a regular basis. Proactively exceed their expectations.

- **Adopting shared goals:** Shared goals amongst subordinates and peers will encourage teamwork as all parties are clear on what is expected of them. In addition, the established shared goals must be granular enough to describe the required tasks to be done by respective parties in order to achieve a common goal. Accordingly, specific performance measures have to be created for the respective parties to serve as continuous improvement process.

- **Giving and taking:** Readiness to give and take will go a long way in nurturing teamwork. In the real world, you always have to do more than the stated scope of work to get things done. When facing situation such as this, focus on the outcomes as that will naturally make you do what's required to get things done indiscriminately. For instance, you are busy trying to get all the sales orders recorded as the cut-off time is at 5pm. While busy making phone calls to your business partners, one of your colleagues comes to you and asks for your help to follow up on her orders as she has a family emergency to attend to. You agree to help despite your huge workload as you appreciate the significance of locking all the orders on that day in order for the department to meet its monthly business forecast. Likewise, the same type of assistance can be expected from any one of the team members whenever circumstances call for it. Giving and taking naturally strengthen your bonding with your team members which benefit you immensely in the long term.

Planning and Organizing

The desired end results of any organizations depend on whether their plans are executed well. Evidently, it is paramount for managers to not only develop good plans, but to ensure that their plans are well executed.

To do this effectively, managers have to have good planning and organizing skills. They must have the ability to:

- Develop plans that detail out key outcomes, milestones, anticipated risks, remedial options and allocation of scheduled resources to achieve objectives within a committed timeframe.
- Assign and authorize relevant personnel to execute the required task at each milestone of the initiative/project plan.
- Proactively anticipate obstacles and methods to overcome them.
- Stay focus at time of crisis.
- Monitor plan progress against target on a regular basis.
- Resolve incompatible needs, requirements and priorities to ensure that initiative/project will complete on time.

Communication

Successful managers have strong communication skills. They adapt to varied audiences and circumstances comfortably. They demonstrate compelling capabilities of:

- Active listening and sending accurate information.
- Influencing and persuading their varied audiences.
- Having deep knowledge and confident in communicating their messages.

- Sharing information with team members and stakeholders to support them on doing their jobs.
- Pursuing information from others.
- Writing and talking briefly, accurately and to the point.

Problem Solving

Managers spend a lot of time solving problems daily. The behavioural skills that reflect excellence in problem solving are indicated by the ability to:

- Identify the existence of the problem.
- Facilitate brainstorming session to come up with solutions.
- Explore potential causes of the problem.
- Determine alternative approaches to resolve the problem.
- Select an approach to resolve the problem.
- Influence participation from other parties in assessing potential solutions to the problems.
- Monitor solution implementation to drive expected results.

Managing Performance for Continuous Improvement

Managers should consider creating an environment that promotes continuous improvement all the time as this will inculcate innovative behaviours among subordinates. Innovative in this scenario means that the subordinates will always be looking for new ways to do things either to improve product offering, enhance customer service or speed up response time to customers.

Promoting continuous improvement to inculcate innovative behaviour means that constant feedback is mandatory. Managers need to deliberately build a structure around giving and receiving feedback such as:

- Appropriate timing and frequency to give feedback.

- Specify rules of engagement, for example, being open and respectful and follow up with prompt actions.

In order to manage performance, managers must work collaboratively together with the subordinates in determining the performance measures. Managers must be able to facilitate the process of determining performance measures in line with the organizational goals and critical success factors.

A key component of managing performance for continuous improvement is incentive. The purpose of incentives is to constantly recognize excellent performers to sustain motivation among team members. The rewards can be in many forms such as two tickets to the current musical show in the city, dinner for two at the best restaurant in town or two tickets to watch Formula One Grand Prix.

Managers need to document the evidence of the outstanding performance clearly. Share it with every team member and the rest of the employees in the organization. Place it on the intranet and treat it as the best practices that team members and other employees can emulate when relevant. This effort will encourage team members to stretch their potentials, always raising the bars.

It is best introduced as periodic initiatives, say quarterly, as this will give ample time for fair assessment. An example of quarterly initiative to a sales team is forecast accuracy within $\pm2\%$ in the relevant quarter.

Action Items for New Managers

Consider the following scenarios. Assess where you stand on each scenario. Work on specific action plans to improve your current situation:

- **Scenario 1:** How do you rate yourself in terms of helping your employees succeed? Have you done enough to create a predictable environment for your team to operate effectively? Work on your department's systemic pulse of operation. Lock in your recurring project/business review meetings, staff meetings, 1:1 meetings and other critical events in your department calendar. Share it with your team members. Communicate the purpose of having such 'unique pulse of operation'. Communicate your expectations and the rules of engagement as well. Execute as planned. Assess how effective such method is in helping your team members succeed. Adjust accordingly based on the results of your assessment.

- **Scenario 2:** How well do you spend your time today? Take stock of how you are spending your time. How much do you spend time on planning? How much on developing? And how much on maintaining? What should you improve on and adjust to ensure that you are investing your time effectively?
- **Scenario 3:** Are you satisfied with the current teamwork in your department? How can you improve the current teamwork even further? What will you do differently in the next thirty to sixty days to improve teamwork in your department?

CORNERSTONE 4:
MANAGING CHANGE

NEW MANAGERS HAVE TO RECOGNIZE and accept that the role of a manager is totally a new territory regardless of how successful they were during their days as individual contributors. The more ready they are to recognize and accept that, the better they will be in coping with the challenges of being managers.

New managers should consider the following approaches to manage the transition from individual contributors to managers:

- **Plan early:** If you want to be a manager, start planning yourself for the role much earlier than your promotion.
- **Establish awareness of what the role is all about:** Scan your organization and observe current managers at work. Pick a "model manager" of your own; someone who impresses you with a good track record and is highly reputable. Take stock of the great qualities that he possesses. Start engaging and learning. Ask questions about where to start in preparing yourself for the role.

- **Engage a coach or mentor:** Once you have established a decent relationship with your "model manager", ask whether he can be your coach or mentor. Communicate your expectation. Likewise, seek his input on the kind of expectation and commitment that he can offer. Take charge of your learning process. Come prepared with focused agenda in every coaching session. Capture what you learn and follow up thoroughly on the agreed action items between you and your coach or mentor.

- **Develop your personal managerial plan:** Constructively work on your personal managerial plan. Do a short term 30.60.90 day plan which basically describes your objectives and action plans within 30, 60 and 90 days. Consider using the Manager's Toolkits as a tool for your preparation. Share the plans with your coach or mentor. Secure his feedback. Update your plans reiteratively upon consultation from your coach or mentor.

- **Seek a trial:** Proactively put a request to be a team leader for some unique project or initiative that requires you practising the managerial skills. This will be a good opportunity to gauge your capabilities and readiness to be a manager.

- **Enhance your plan:** Upon completion of your trial, capture your experience from three perspectives: what's working, what's not and what should be done differently. Update your managerial plan. Keep on updating whenever you learn something new.

Assuming that you receive your promotion to become a manager without your expecting it and you have to assume the role within a reasonably quick timeframe and you believe that you will be able to fulfill such role, you can consider the following approach:

- **Speak with the current manager holding the position that you are supposed to fulfil to discuss these:**

  o Vision, strategic objectives, critical success factors, key priorities, current problems and challenges of the department.

- o Immediate and future plans.
- o Assessment of human capital, skill sets, capabilities and competencies.
- o Strengths, weaknesses, opportunities and threats (SWOT) of the team.
- o State of teamwork and cross group collaboration.

- **Speak with your future direct manager and discuss these:**

  - o His expectations of the department in relation to its contribution to the organization.
  - o His perceived strengths, weaknesses, opportunities and threats (SWOT) of the department.
  - o His immediate and future plans.
  - o His key priorities.
  - o What he thinks should be done differently.

- **Mutually develop a joint plan with your direct manager for your first 100 days as a manager:**

  - o Develop a plan for your first 100 days as a manager.
  - o Be sure to incorporate the feedback of both (the current manager and your future direct manager) in your plan.
  - o Discuss your plan with your future direct manager and seek his feedback.
  - o Update your plan to incorporate his further views and feedback.
  - o Agree on a suitable method of monitoring the execution of the plan with your future direct manager.

- **Update and enhance the plan on a periodic basis:**

  - o Treat the plan as a living document.
  - o Execute on it.

o Incorporate new development and activities as required suitably over time.

o Seek your direct manager's feedback on a regular basis.

The above approach will prepare you for the role of being a manager. You will walk into the role with a high degree of awareness on the exact opportunities and challenges that the role represents. You recognize that you have to change your working methods. The support from your coaches, mentors, and future direct managers at the onset will help you a great deal in embracing, adapting and managing change associated with the transition from an individual contributor to a successful manager.

Action Items for New Managers

Help yourself manage your transition from an individual contributor to a manager by keeping a weekly journal to monitor your comfort level in discharging your managerial role. Focus on three key areas as listed below:

- **Scenario 1:** Do the members of your team know how to work with you? You can start by sharing with them your work or management style. Be very open about it. State your hot buttons, your likes and dislikes and the best approach to work together for optimal results. Convey your expectations of each one of them. Ask them about their expectations of you as well. Upon doing this, observe the progress of your relationship with your team members gradually over time. Capture specific situations that require improvement. Execute the required improvement. Repeat observations and improvements continually.

- **Scenario 2:** How well are you collaborating with your peers? Have you tried to get to know your peers? Have you spent some time engaging with them, exchanging ideas on how best to support each other for a common purpose in alignment with your organization's goal? Have you shared your key priorities with them? Have you understood their needs and requirements to enable them to support you effectively? Assess where you stand and work on collaborating effectively with your peers.

- **Scenario 3:** Does your department have a positive image? Do you know whether your organization have a positive perception of your team? Do you know how your direct manager and peers perceive your team? Are they impressed? Are they respectful? In what area should you improve? Find out their perceptions regularly. Understand why certain perceptions are formed. Work on improving the areas that need improvement on a regular basis.

PART 2

The Manager's Toolkits

THE MANAGER'S TOOLKITS OVERVIEW

THE MANAGER'S TOOLKITS ARE A set of preparatory and assessment tools for managers to use in readying themselves to take up the role of first time managers and to take stock of their current performance as managers.

The Manager's Toolkits consist of two components, namely, imManager Framework and imManager Guide. They work hand in glove together.

How Do You Use the Manager's Toolkits?

You will achieve maximum benefits when you use the toolkits as follows:

- Gain understanding of the imManager Framework first.
- Start your evaluation and assessment from the top to bottom of the framework.
- Go through the questionnaires in the imManager Guide in the same sequence as the framework.

- Capture your assessment in the imManager Guide.
- Have your own summary on the overall action plans that you will pursue in the future.
- Execute your plan as documented.

imMANAGER FRAMEWORK

The imManager framework is a diagnostic execution plan that helps managers prepare their readiness to undertake the managerial role for the first time, assess where they stand at any one point in time in relation to the expected scope of a managerial role and sustain their stay on course of being a manager.

The purposes of the imManager Framework include assisting first time managers to focus on the right things, serving as a roadmap to lead and manage team and encourage managers to ask the hard questions in their pursuit to develop high performing teams.

The imManager Framework diagram is depicted below:

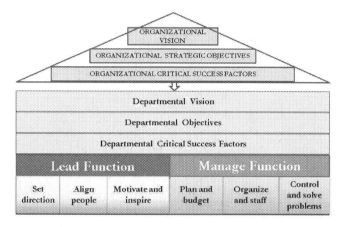

Diagram 4: imManager Framework

The design principle of the imManager framework is diagnostic rather than prescriptive and the accompanying imManager Guide serves as the guidelines during the diagnostic process.

The accompanying imManager Guide consists of a checklist questions format for each section of the imManager Framework, as depicted below:

Section of the imManager Framework	Categories of checklists in the imManager Guide
Organizational Level	• Vision • Strategic Objectives • Critical Success Factors
Departmental Level	• Vision • Strategic Objectives • Critical Success Factors
Lead Function	• Set Direction • Align People • Motivate and Inspire
Manage Function	• Plan and Budget • Organize and Staff • Control and Solve Problems

Details of the questionnaires for each category of the checklists are illustrated in the imManager Guide section.

Organizational Level: Vision, Strategic Objectives and Critical Success Factors

Let us understand the big picture first by understanding the organizational level vision, strategic objectives and critical success factors. These must be fully understood as they:

- Indicate the future state that the organization aspires to be in.
- Steer the organization to focus on the right objectives to be successful.
- Prioritize the characteristics, conditions and variables that have direct and high impact on the organization's effectiveness, efficiency and viability.

Vision

Vision can be defined as an inspirational description of what an organization would like to achieve or accomplish in the midterm or long term future[8].

It is intended to serve as a clear guide for choosing current and future course of action[8].

Microsoft's vision in the first 25 years of its establishment, for example, was a personal computer on every desk in every home. After 25 years, its vision was empowering people through great software anytime, anyplace and on any device. Its most current vision is helping people and businesses throughout the world to realize their full potential.

Vision therefore, can change with time in response to market changes and the defined strategy that the organization undertakes to stay relevant.

Strategic Objectives

Strategic objectives are broadly defined objectives that an organization must achieve to make its strategy succeed[9].

They are externally focused and according to Peter Drucker, fall into eight major classifications: market standing, innovation, human resource, financial resource, physical resource, productivity, social responsibility and profit requirements[9]. Some examples of strategic objectives are:

- **Profit requirements:** Achieve 2 billion in annual revenue with 120 million in profit.
- **Human resource:** Have a complete management team.
- **Physical resources**: Have a comprehensive technology development and implementation plan.

Critical Success Factors

Critical Success Factors (CSFs) can be defined as limited number (usually between 3 and 8) of characteristics, conditions or variables that have a direct and serious impact on the effectiveness, efficiency and viability of an organization, program or project[10]. Some examples of CSFs are:

- **CSF for Finance**: Reducing supply chain cost.
- **CSF for Customer:** Delivery in full on time, all the time to our key customers.
- **CSF for internal process:** Finding better ways to do the things we do every day.
- **CSF for learning and growth:** Innovative ideas from staff encouraged and adopted quickly.

Departmental Level: Vision, Strategic Objectives and Critical Success Factors

Based on the organizational level vision, strategic objectives and CSFs perform the following at the departmental level:

- Evaluate and assess how the department contributes to the overall organizational requirements.
- Determine degree of impact for each relevant contribution.
- Prioritize based on the degree of impact.
- Develop vision, strategic objectives and critical success factors for the department in alignment with the organizational level.
- Validate the alignment between department and the organizational level.

Lead Function: Set Direction, Align People, Motivate and Inspire

Microsoft, in 1995, demonstrated a very strong lead function when it had to catch up with the then, reputable Internet leader, Netscape. After enjoying an unprecedented growth in the software market for two decades with its flagship product, Windows, it was hard for Microsoft to appreciate the real threat of Internet, even when Netscape had so much traction on its Netscape Navigator internet browser.

That situation changed dramatically when Netscape launched its initial public offering and its price soared from USD28 to USD58 on the very day it was listed, which triggered the bull market of Internet stocks[11].

Bill Gates, the Founder and CEO of Microsoft at that point in time, issued the infamous Internet Tidal Wave memo detailing out that the threat of the Internet was real and Microsoft might not be relevant unless drastic actions were taken and executed fast. His message coupled with the soaring price of Internet stocks created so much fear among Microsoft employees that everyone was just ready to embrace change and execute.

Within such a short time, Microsoft communicated the strategy to all the employees via many channels such as group meetings, email, videos and closed circuit TV. Product groups started integrating the Internet capabilities into all their product developments. Microsoft acquired some Internet companies such as Velmeer Technology (which carried FrontPage development tool). Strategic alliance with key market leader such as American On Line (AOL) was established where Microsoft granted AOL free world-wide distribution rights to Internet Explorer and likewise, Microsoft agreed to distribute AOL's proprietary access software in Windows and to place an AOL icon in the OLS folder on the Windows desktop[12].

As a result of the effective leadership and rapid actions taken, Microsoft was able to offer innovative solutions and compelling computing experience as demanded by the consumers.

In a nutshell, Microsoft did the following very effectively as far as the lead function is concerned:

Lead Function	What was done
Set direction	Embrace and extend Internet capability in every product.
Align people	Multi tiered communications on strategy at every level, create sense of urgency to embrace change, invest in new partnerships and alliances, provide the environment and tools for the employees to excel in the new strategic direction.
Motivate and inspire	Increased valuation of Internet stocks, genuine fear of losing to competitors, passion to stay relevant in the software market and lead the industry.

Manage Function: Plan and Budget, Organize and Staff, Control and Solve Problem

The three components of the manage function and their objectives are:

Manage Function	Objectives
Plan and budget	To enhance business predictability and deliver results in alignment with corporate vision.
Organize and staff	To provide the required environment, resources and capabilities (skills, knowledge, right attitude) in order to deliver the desired results.
Control and solve problems	To sustain continuous operations and improvements in meeting customers and stakeholders' expectations by balancing trade-offs.

The key activities involved in the manage function are listed, but not limited to, below:

Manage Function	Key Activities
Plan and Budget	1. Revisit business goals for the relevant financial year. 2. Determine strategic initiatives to achieve business goals. 3. Develop execution plan for each strategic initiative complete with timeline, required resources and skill sets, detailed tasks and responsibilities. 4. Develop yearly budget and schedule of budget expenses to support execution plan.
Organize and Staff	1. Establish organizational and staffing plan to support execution plan based on the allocated budget and schedule of expenses. 2. Hire the required resources as planned. 3. Facilitate learning and development required to enhance staff skill sets. 4. Discuss and establish role-based performance measures. 5. Coach staffs as required.
Control and Solve Problem	1. Periodic progress review of strategic initiatives, execution and budget plans. 2. Periodic checkpoints with staffs on their performances. 3. Follow up on outstanding open issues till closure. 4. Allocate some small percentage of time for potential ad-hoc issues that may arise.

imMANAGER GUIDE

ImMANAGER GUIDE IS A CHECKLIST of questionnaires that is used to diagnose one's position within each component of the imManager Framework.

You have to assess yourself by going through each question and documenting your answers in the status, statement and action items column. Upon completion, you can summarize your overall action plans in the summary page.

Details of the imManager Guide are listed below:

PART 1: ORGANIZATIONAL LEVEL				
Item	Description	Status	Statement	Action Items
1.1	Do I understand the vision of my organization?	☐ Yes ☐ No		

Item	Description	Status	Statement	Action Items
1.2	Do I understand the strategic objectives of my organization?	☐ Yes ☐ No		
1.3	Do I understand the critical success factors of my organization?	☐ Yes ☐ No		
1.4	Which success factors will be directly relevant to my department?			
1.5	Do I understand the current financial year strategic initiatives?	☐ Yes ☐ No		
1.6	Which strategic initiatives will be directly relevant to my department?			

Item	Description	Status	Statement	Action Items
1.7	Which strategic initiatives will be shared among many departments?			
1.8	Which departments share the same strategic initiatives with my department?			
1.9	Based on the shared strategic initiatives, what kind of shared goals should I establish with the relevant department?			

Item	Description	Status	Statement	Action Items
PART 2: DEPARTMENTAL LEVEL				
2.1	What is my vision for my department?			
2.2	What does success look like to my department?			
2.3	Where does my department stand today in relation to my vision?			
2.4	What is my honest assessment of my team currently? (Evaluate strengths, weaknesses, opportunities and threats (SWOT))			
2.5	Can my current team at the current capabilities achieve the desired success?	☐ Yes ☐ No		

Item	Description	Status	Statement	Action Items
2.6	What are the shared goals of my department? (refers to the different roles in your own department)			
2.7	How do I measure success of my department?			

PART 3A: LEAD FUNCTION				
3A.1: SET DIRECTION				
Item	Description	Status	Statement	Action items
3A.1.1	Have I prepared a planned communication structure to effectively communicate with my team?	☐ Yes ☐ No		
3A.1.2	Have I communicated the organization's vision, critical success factors and strategic initiatives to my team?	☐ Yes ☐ No		
3A.1.3	Does my team have full clarity on the organization's vision, critical success factors and strategic initiatives?	☐ Yes ☐ No		

Item	Description	Status	Statement	Action items
3A.1.4	Have I engaged my team and communicate the following about the department effectively? • What success looks like? • How success is measured? • Its shared goals. • Assessment of team capabilities. • My expectations of the team.	☐ Yes ☐ No		
3A.1.5	Does my team have the understanding of how to work together effectively and what is expected of them?	☐ Yes ☐ No		

3A.2: ALIGN PEOPLE				
Item	Description	Status	Statement	Action items
3A.2.1	Do I have clear action plans on how to influence change among my team members?	☐ Yes ☐ No		
3A.2.2	Do I have good 'change evangelist' within my team to help demonstrate the benefits of change?	☐ Yes ☐ No		
3A.2.3	Have I listened enough to my team's concerns and their reluctance to change?	☐ Yes ☐ No		
3A.2.4	Have I done the right thing to address my team's concerns and their reluctance to change?	☐ Yes ☐ No		

Item	Description	Status	Statement	Action items
3A.2.5	Do I need my direct manager to be involved in addressing my team's concerns and reluctance to change?	□ Yes □ No		
3A.2.6	Do I need other forms of interventions to address my team's concerns and reluctance to change?	□ Yes □ No		

3A.3: MOTIVATE AND INSPIRE

Item	Description	Status	Statement	Action items
3A.3.1	Is my team motivated and inspired?	□ Yes □ No		
3A.3.2	Do I have structured ongoing recognition plans/ activities for my team?	□ Yes □ No		
3A.3.3	Do I know my team's employee satisfaction level today?	□ Yes □ No		
3A.3.4	Do I have a reliable method to assess my team's employee satisfaction level?	□ Yes □ No		
3A.3.5	Have I inculcated a healthy work culture among my team members?	□ Yes □ No		

Item	Description	Status	Statement	Action items
3A.3.6	Have I inculcated a good working environment for my team?	☐ Yes ☐ No		

PART 3B: MANAGE FUNCTION				
3B.1: PLAN AND BUDGET				
Item	**Description**	**Status**	**Statement**	**Action items**
3B.1.1	Based on how success looks like, have I crafted a detailed plan on how to achieve that?	□ Yes □ No		
3B.1.2	Have I identified the key strategic initiatives for this financial year?	□ Yes □ No		
3B.1.3	Have I detailed out the key activities within each strategic initiative and the planned dates for the relevant activities?	□ Yes □ No		
3B.1.4	Have I quantified the required resources (man, material, money) to execute the planned activities?	□ Yes □ No		

Item	Description	Status	Statement	Action items
3B.1.5	Have I prepared the corresponding budget required to execute the agreed initiatives?	☐ Yes ☐ No		
3B.1.6	Have I identified the required resources to execute the agreed initiatives?	☐ Yes ☐ No		
3B.1.7	Do I have the relevant capabilities to execute the agreed initiatives?	☐ Yes ☐ No		
3B.1.8	Have I acquired the relevant capabilities to execute the agreed initiatives?	☐ Yes ☐ No		

Item	Description	Status	Statement	Action items
3B.1.9	Have I identified the associated risk in all of these strategic initiatives?	□ Yes □ No		
3B.1.10	Have I built enough contingency plans to mitigate the associated risk?	□ Yes □ No		
3B.1.11	Have I allocated the additional budget associated with the identified risk factors in these initiatives?	□ Yes □ No		

3B.2: ORGANIZE AND STAFF				
Item	Description	Status	Statement	Action items
3B.2.1	Have I engaged and communicated with my team about my department's performance goals?	☐ Yes ☐ No		
3B.2.2	Have I engaged with each one of my team members and discussed about our mutual expectations?	☐ Yes ☐ No		
3B.2.3	Have I provided my team members the department unit pulse of operation calendar? (An example of systemic pulse of operations can be found in Cornerstone 3: Behaviour Skills under the topic of Helping Employees Succeed).	☐ Yes ☐ No		

Item	Description	Status	Statement	Action items
3B.2.4	Have I engaged with my team and discussed about the performance management and assessment cycle?	☐ Yes ☐ No		
3B.2.5	Have I fixed the recurring time and frequency for my department meetings?	☐ Yes ☐ No		
3B.2.6	Have I fixed the recurring time and frequency for my 30 minute 1:1 meetings with my subordinates?	☐ Yes ☐ No		
3B.2.7	Have I worked with HR to develop the New Hire On boarding program for my new hires?	☐ Yes ☐ No		

Item	Description	Status	Statement	Action items
3B.2.8	Have I discussed with my team members on their learning and development needs?	☐ Yes ☐ No		
3B.2.9	Have I coached my team members on developing their performance goals?	☐ Yes ☐ No		
3B.2.10	Have I coached my team members on taking charge of their own performance?	☐ Yes ☐ No		

3B.3: CONTROL AND SOLVE PROBLEMS				
Item	**Description**	**Status**	**Statement**	**Action items**
3B.3.1	Are my team members executing well as per planned targets?	□ Yes □ No		
3B.3.2	Have I fulfilled all my 30 minute 1:1 session once a fortnight with each of my team member?	□ Yes □ No		
3B.3.3	Have I fulfilled all the required commitments in the department pulse of operation? (An example of systemic pulse of operations can be found in Cornerstone 3: Behaviour Skills under the topic of Helping Employees Succeed).	□ Yes □ No		

Item	Description	Status	Statement	Action items
3B.3.4	Am I aware of the top three issues right now?	□ Yes □ No		
3B.3.5	Have I taken the necessary steps to speedily resolve the top three issues?	□ Yes □ No		
3B.3.6	Have I discussed the performance progress of my team members on a monthly basis?	□ Yes □ No		
3B.3.7	Am I able to hire new employees as per planned schedule?	□ Yes □ No		
3B.3.8	Have I been spending the allocated marketing budget as per planned schedule?	□ Yes □ No		

Item	Description	Status	Statement	Action items
3B.3.9	Do I have any great talents leaving the company?	□ Yes □ No		
3B.3.10	Do I know the reasons why great talents leave the company?	□ Yes □ No		
3B.3.11	Do I know the reasons why great talents stay with the company?	□ Yes □ No		
3B.3.12	Do I communicate objectively to poor performers highlighting their performance against expectation and constructively engage to understand their issues?	□ Yes □ No		

Item	Description	Status	Statement	Action items
3B.3.13	Do I coach the poor performers and agree on specific deliverables on a timely basis?	□ Yes □ No		

SUMMARY OF ACTION PLANS

B<small>ASED ON THE ASSESSMENT</small>, MY 30.60.90 day summary of action plans are:

Name of Manager:		Date of Assessment:	
Time	Activities	Ownership	Attendees
30 days			
60 days			
90 days			

APPENDIX

Personal Managerial Plan

THIS SECTION DETAILS OUT AN example of a personal managerial plan using the imManager Toolkits. This will help new managers visualize the application of the imManager Toolkits and how they can assist them in planning and assessing their own managerial tasks.

A snapshot of a personal managerial plan of Johan's, a sales manager working with a business application solution organization in the field of Client Relationship Management (CRM) is depicted below.

PART 1: ORGANIZATIONAL LEVEL				
Item	Description	Status	Statement	Action Items
1.1	Do I understand the vision of my organization?	√ Yes □ No	*Shared with team members last month.*	

Item	Description	Status	Statement	Action Items
1.2	Do I understand the strategic objectives of my organization?	√ Yes ☐ No	*Shared with team members last month.*	
1.3	Do I understand the critical success factors of my organization?	√ Yes ☐ No	*Shared with team members last month.*	
1.4	Which success factors will be directly relevant to my department?		*CSF for finance: Increase share of wallet of top ten customers.* *CSF for customer: Enhance satisfaction of key customers* *CSF for internal process: finding better ways to do the things we do every day* *CSF for learning and growth: innovative ideas from staff encouraged and adopted quickly*	*Communicate CSFs to my team members.*

Item	Description	Status	Statement	Action Items
1.5	Do I understand the current financial year strategic initiatives?	√ Yes □ No	*Telco industry as new target segment. Winning and maintaining current installed base with the new CRM Version 5.0. Increase customer and partner satisfaction by 5 points.*	*Strengthen message with team members.*
1.6	Which strategic initiatives will be directly relevant to my department?		*Leverage growth in the telco industry, 10% uptake in the latest CRM Version 5.0; establish strategic alliance with the top three local systems integrator.*	*Communicate strategic initiatives to my team members.*
1.7	Which strategic initiatives will be shared among many departments?		*Leverage growth in the telco industry, 10% uptake in the latest CRM Version 5.0.*	*Communicate details with my team members.*

Item	Description	Status	Statement	Action Items
1.8	Which departments share the same strategic initiatives with my department?		*Consulting and Premier Support.*	*Initiate a meeting with both the Head of Consulting and Premier Support.*
1.9	Based on the shared strategic initiatives, what kind of shared goals should I establish with the relevant department?		*To win one key opportunity in the telco industry to include fee-based service of the consulting and premier support team.*	*To discuss this proposed shared goals with Consulting and Premier Support.*

PART 2: DEPARTMENTAL LEVEL				
Item	Description	Status	Statement	Action Items
2.1	What is my vision for my department?		*To be the leading CRM solution provider in the local market and contribute 40% of the total revenue of the organization.*	*Communicate vision to my team members.*
2.2	What does success look like to my department?		*Acquire one new account in the telecommunications industry.* *30% of the current installed base upgrade to CRM Version 5.0.* *Healthy pipeline (three times the value of planned revenue) of CRM opportunities.*	*Engage with team members to discuss and share what success looks like to the department.*

Item	Description	Status	Statement	Action Items
2.3	Where does my department stand today in relation to my vision?		*On a scale of 1 to 5 (1 being poor and 5 being excellent), my department is a 3 as 20% of pipelines are suspect and the headcount for telecommunication is yet to be hired.*	*Weekly scrub of pipeline during weekly sales meetings, discuss with HR on the possibility of introducing referrals for hire and appoint additional head hunters to speed up identification of potential hires.*

Item	Description	Status	Statement	Action Items
2.4	What is my honest assessment of my team currently? (Evaluate strengths, weaknesses, opportunities and threats (SWOT))		***Strengths:*** *Insurance and banking industry are solid. Experienced account managers with strong industry back up* ***Weaknesses:*** *Telco is a new industry. Still looking for the right hire* ***Opportunities:*** *Growth in telco is new revenue opportunities; new product CRM Version 5.0 is low hanging fruits for the installed base of V3.0 and V4.0.* ***Threats:*** *Well established CRM solution and software as a service providers are aggressive and getting tractions in the local market.*	*Explore strategic partnership with leading local systems integrators in the telco industry, introduce holistic campaign on the benefits of CRM Version 5.0 in relation to the established brands and the software as a service providers, special upgrade program for current installed base of Version 3.0 and 4.0.*

Item	Description	Status	Statement	Action Items
2.5	Can my current team at the current capabilities achieve the desired success?	□ Yes √ No	*Telco industry resource need to be hired soonest, strategic partnership with the leading local system integrators in the telco industry needs to happen, support roadmap from the consulting and premier support for the telco industry need to be established and agreed.*	*Hire the right resource to handle telco industry, shortlist potential local systems integrators to partner with, meet up with Head of Consulting and Premier Support to establish the support roadmap and packages for the telco industry.*
2.6	What are the shared goals of my department? (refers to the different roles in your own department)		*Account Manager and Technical Pre Sales:* *Win CRM Version 5.0 in new accounts.* *Win CRM Version 5.0 Upgrade in current installed base.*	*To communicate to team members*

Item	Description	Status	Statement	Action Items
2.7	How do I measure success of my department?		*Win one new account in telco industry.* *30% of installed base upgrade to CRM Version 5.0.* *5 points increase in customer and partner satisfaction.*	*To communicate success measurement to team members.*

PART 3A: LEAD FUNCTION				
3A.1: SET DIRECTION				
Item	Description	Status	Statement	Action items
3A.1.1	Have I prepared a planned communication structure to effectively communicate with my team?	√ Yes □ No	*Planned channels of communication include face-to-face, sales meeting session, 1:1 session, emails and open door policy.*	*To share with my team members on the various channels and objective of each. Seek feedback as well.*
3A.1.2	Have I communicated the organization's vision, critical success factors and strategic initiatives to my team?	√ Yes □ No	*While this has been done before, it is time to refresh and gauge team understanding of the whole thing. Also the addition of some new members calls for a refresher to ensure that everyone is on the same page.*	*To fix a meeting next week to communicate with my team on details of this.*

Item	Description	Status	Statement	Action items
3A.1.3	Does my team have full clarity on the organization's vision, critical success factors and strategic initiatives?	□ Yes □ No	*Refer statement above. Time to gauge and reassess.*	*To fix a meeting next week to communicate with my team on details of this.*
3A.1.4	Have I engaged my team and communicate the following about the department effectively? • What success looks like? • How success is measured? • Its shared goals. • Assessment of team capabilities. • My expectations of the team.	□ Yes √ No	*I have not done this extensively involving everyone.*	*To share details of these with my team in the next meeting.*

Item	Description	Status	Statement	Action items
3A.1.5	Does my team have the understanding of how to work together effectively and what is expected of them?	☐ Yes √No	*Sporadically yes, but on the overall this needs to be revisited especially with the new addition to the team.*	*Will cover this topic in the meeting next week.*

3A.2: ALIGN PEOPLE				
Item	Description	Status	Statement	Action items
3A.2.1	Do I have clear action plans on how to influence change among my team members?	□ Yes √ No	*Current action plans are not effective. 60% of the team members have not completed their account plans yet*	*To consider new approach of prioritizing resources to those who have completed account plans.*
3A.2.2	Do I have good change evangelist within my team to help demonstrate the benefits of change?	√ Yes □ No	*David is a good potential to become the change evangelist. He completed good and effective account plans for his accounts.*	*Will speak with David and bounce off the idea of getting him to be the change evangelist.*
3A.2.3	Have I listened enough to my team's concerns and their reluctance to change?	√ Yes □ No	*Not enough time in a day seems to be the reason as they need to be out in the field to see clients.*	*Keep on showing the benefits of account plans. Seek best practices.*

Item	Description	Status	Statement	Action items
3A.2.4	Have I done the right thing to address my team's concerns and their reluctance to change?	□ Yes √ No	*Have to start addressing it now.*	*To discuss with David and finalize a collective approach to help the team.*
3A.2.5	Do I need my direct manager to be involved in addressing my team's concerns and reluctance to change?	□ Yes √ No	*Will work on the approach with David first at this juncture. If it doesn't work then will get my direct manager involve within the next four weeks.*	
3A.2.6	Do I need other forms of interventions to address my team's concerns and reluctance to change?	□ Yes √ No		

Item	Description	Status	Statement	Action items
3A.3: MOTIVATE AND INSPIRE				
3A.3.1	Is my team motivated and inspired?	☐ Yes ☐ No	*70% are motivated and inspired. 30% may not be.*	*Validate the level of motivation of the 30%.*
3A.3.2	Do I have structured ongoing recognition plans / activities for my team?	√ Yes ☐ No		
3A.3.3	Do I know my team's employee satisfaction level today?	☐ Yes √ No	*Have never done or assess employee satisfaction to date.*	*Will work on a simple way of assessing satisfaction level.*
3A.3.4	Do I have a reliable method to assess my team's employee satisfaction level?	☐ Yes √ No	*Have never done or assess employee satisfaction to date.*	*Will evaluate a few methods that other organizations utilize.*

Item	Description	Status	Statement	Action items
3A.3.5	Have I inculcated a healthy work culture among my team members?	√ Yes □ No		
3A.3.6	Have I inculcated a good working environment for my team?	√ Yes □ No		

PART 3B: MANAGE FUNCTION				
3B.1: PLAN AND BUDGET				
Item	Description	Status	Statement	Action items
3B.1.1	Based on how success looks like, have I crafted a detailed plan on how to achieve that?	√ Yes ☐ No	*Discussed with my team members two weeks ago.*	
3B.1.2	Have I identified the key strategic initiatives for this financial year?	√ Yes ☐ No	*Win one new account in telco.* *30% revenue from CRM Version 5.0 upgrade in the current installed base. Partner with leading local integrator in one strategic account.*	
3B.1.3	Have I detailed out the key activities within each strategic initiative and the planned dates for the relevant activities?	√ Yes ☐ No		*To share with direct manager, Head of Consulting and Premier Support on the detail activities.*

Item	Description	Status	Statement	Action items
3B.1.4	Have I quantified the required resources (man, material, money) to execute the planned activities?	√ Yes □ No		*Will walk through details of the overall quantified resources with direct manager, Head of Consulting and Premier Support.*
3B.1.5	Have I prepared the corresponding budget required to execute the agreed initiatives?	√ Yes □ No	*Need to discuss with my direct manager to seek his feedback on the budget.*	*To fix a meeting with my direct manager to discuss details.*
3B.1.6	Have I identified the required resources to execute the agreed initiatives?	□ Yes √ No	*Need to finalize with my team members on the agreed initiatives and the identification of the required resources.*	*To discuss with team members on initiatives and identification of resources.*

Item	Description	Status	Statement	Action items
3B.1.7	Do I have the relevant capabilities to execute the agreed initiatives?	□ Yes √ No	*Not fully. Two initiatives require specialist skills not available locally.*	*To validate with the Consulting department on specialist skills availabilities and where to source from.*
3B.1.8	Have I acquired the relevant capabilities to execute the agreed initiatives?	□ Yes √ No	*Approach based on priorities. Focus on required capabilities for initiatives in this quarter first.*	*To discuss with technical support and consulting department on prioritization of resources and their availabilities.*
3B.1.9	Have I identified the associated risk in all of these strategic initiatives?	√ Yes □ No	*Incorporated 20% risk factor on each initiative.*	*Will pass to technical support and consulting to vet further.*

Item	Description	Status	Statement	Action items
3B.1.10	Have I built enough contingency plans to mitigate the associated risk?	√ Yes □ No		*Will seek feedback from technical support and consulting as well.*
3B.1.11	Have I allocated the additional budget associated with the identified risk factors in these initiatives?	□ Yes √ No	*Not enough budget*	*Will discuss with technical support and consulting on how best to reduce the risk.*

3B.2: ORGANIZE AND STAFF				
Item	Description	Status	Statement	Action items
3B.2.1	Have I engaged and communicated with my team about my department's performance goals?	√ Yes □ No	*The team felt that the revenue numbers were ambitious.*	*To project the qualified prospects to justify the numbers for their agreement.*
3B.2.2	Have I engaged with each one of my team members and discussed about our mutual expectations?	□ Yes √ No	*Completed 60% of the team so far.*	*Will continue with the other 40% early next week.*
3B.2.3	Have I provided my team members the department unit pulse of operation calendar? (An example of systemic pulse of operations can be found in Cornerstone 3: Behaviour Skills under the topic of Helping Employees Succeed).	√ Yes □ No	*Going on well.*	

Item	Description	Status	Statement	Action items
3B.2.4	Have I engaged with my team and discussed about the performance management and assessment cycle?	□ Yes √ No	*Process of seeking feedback and concerns from the team right now.*	*Will fix a date to conduct this session with team members. Target three weeks from now.*
3B.2.5	Have I fixed the recurring time and frequency for my department meetings?	√ Yes □ No	*Going on well.*	
3B.2.6	Have I fixed the recurring time and frequency for my 30 minute 1:1 meetings with my subordinates?	√ Yes □ No	*Going on well.*	
3B.2.7	Have I worked with HR to develop the New Hire On boarding program for my new hires?	□ Yes √ No	*Expect to get new hires in 60 days.*	*Will discuss the program with HR next month.*

Item	Description	Status	Statement	Action items
3B.2.8	Have I discussed with my team members on their learning and development needs?	√ Yes □ No	*Work in progress. Has asked them to come up with their proposed plans.*	*Will discuss in my 1:1 session with the team members as per fixed schedules.*
3B.2.9	Have I coached my team members on developing their performance goals?	√ Yes □ No	*Done during my 1:1 sessions.*	*Follow up on their drafts of performance goals.*
3B.2.10	Have I coached my team members on taking charge of their own performance?	√ Yes □ No	*Done during my 1:1 sessions.*	*Follow up on their drafts of performance goals.*

3B.3: CONTROL AND SOLVE PROBLEMS				
Item	Description	Status	Statement	Action items
3B.3.1	Are my team members executing well as per planned targets?	□ Yes √ No	*20% are below par.*	*To coach and monitor closely on progress of the 20%.*
3B.3.2	Have I fulfilled all my 30 minute 1:1 session once a fortnight with each of my team member?	√ Yes □ No	*Going on well.*	
3B.3.3	Have I fulfilled all the required commitments in the department pulse of operation? (An example of systemic pulse of operations can be found in Cornerstone 3: Behaviour Skills under the topic of Helping Employees Succeed).	√ Yes □ No	*Going on well.*	

Item	Description	Status	Statement	Action items
3B.3.4	Am I aware of the top three issues right now?	√ Yes □ No	*20% are not executing well. Lack of skilled capabilities in two strategic initiatives. Change to the new sales culture is not satisfactory.*	*Discuss with my direct manager and tighten monitoring process on these.*
3B.3.5	Have I taken the necessary steps to speedily resolve the top three issues?	√ Yes □ No	*Coach the 20% on what to prioritize and execute based on weekly schedules. Sourcing for skilled resources has started with the help from Consulting and Technical Support. Showcase David's work and success story in adopting the new approach of selling.*	*Follow up on these three initiatives on a weekly basis.*
3B.3.6	Have I discussed the performance progress of my team members on a monthly basis?	√ Yes □ No	*Going on well.*	

Item	Description	Status	Statement	Action items
3B.3.7	Am I able to hire new employees as per planned schedule?	√ Yes □ No	*Interviews have started. Target hiring in 60 days.*	
3B.3.8	Have I been spending the allocated marketing budget as per planned schedule?	√ Yes □ No	*So far going on as planned.*	
3B.3.9	Do I have any great talents leaving the company?	□ Yes √ No		
3B.3.10	Do I know the reasons why great talents leave the company?	□ Yes √ No	*Within my team, I have not had any loss of talents yet.*	
3B.3.11	Do I know the reasons why great talents stay with the company?	√ Yes □ No	*Competitive compensation in the industry. Employees feel appreciated.*	

Item	Description	Status	Statement	Action items
3B.3.12	Do I communicate objectively to poor performers highlighting their performance against expectation and constructively engage to understand their issues?	□ Yes √ No		*To communicate about their performance against expectations and agree on collective action plans in my next 1:1 meeting.*
3B.3.13	Do I coach the poor performers and agree on specific deliverables on a timely basis?	√ Yes □ No	*While agreement on deliverables is achieved, monitoring process is not satisfactory.*	*Will start monitoring progress and activities to ensure deliverables are met.*

Summary of Action Plans

Based on the assessment, my 30.60.90 day summary of action plans are:

Name of Manager: Johan S.		Date of Assessment: March 15th, 2012	
Time	Activities	Ownership	Attendees
30 days	Communicate organization's CSFs, strategic initiatives and shared strategic initiatives to team members to confirm clarity, understanding and seek feedback.	Johan	All team members.
30 days	Meet with Head of Consulting and Premier Support to discuss proposed shared goals.	Johan	Head of Consulting and Premier Support.

Time	Activities	Ownership	Attendees
30 days	*Communicate department's vision and success measurements with team members. Seek feedback and agreement on success measurements.*	*Johan*	*All team members.*
30 days	*Discuss with Head of Consulting and Premier Support on the support roadmap for CRM Version 5.0.*	*Johan*	*Head of Consulting and Premier Support.*
30 days	*Discuss structured communication channels, department's vision, strategic objectives, CSFs, what success looks like, success measurements, team capabilities and mutual expectations.*	*Johan*	*All team members.*

Time	Activities	Ownership	Attendees
30 days	*Walk through the details of quantified resources for each strategic initiative for the department to seek agreement on resource allocation and budget.*	*Johan*	*Direct Manager, Head of Consulting and Premier Support, Head of Product Marketing.*
30 days	*Scrub pipelines in the weekly sales meeting.*	*Johan*	*All team members.*
60 days	*Discuss with HR on the methods to identify potential hires effectively. (for example, referrals and head hunters).*	*Johan*	*Head of HR.*
60 days	*Initiate meetings with potential local integrators. Call the top three local integrators for appointments.*	*Johan*	*Top three local integrators.*

Time	Activities	Ownership	Attendees
60 days	*Discuss with product marketing team to develop CRM campaign and special upgrade programs.*	*Johan*	*Head of Product Marketing.*
60 days	*Communicate with team members on new ways of prioritizing allocation of resources which will be based on completion of account plans.*	*Johan*	*Via email to all team members.*
60 days	*Meet with David to discuss his role as a change agent to influence the rest of the team members to adopt the new sales approach. Develop best practices of the new sales approach to showcase benefits.*	*Johan*	*David*

Time	Activities	Ownership	Attendees
60 days	*Discuss mutual expectations, learning and development plan and follow up on drafts of performance goals.*	*Johan*	*All team members.*
60 days	*Scrub pipelines in the weekly sales meeting.*	*Johan*	*All team members.*
90 days	*Meet with team members to discuss the new initiative to encourage adoption of the new sales approach and incentive to complete the account plans.*	*Johan*	*All team members.*
90 days	*Evaluate methods to assess level of employee satisfaction.*	*Johan*	*Head of HR.*
90 days	*Develop a simple way of assessing employee satisfaction level.*	*Head of HR*	

Time	Activities	Ownership	Attendees
90 days	*Engage with team members to discuss performance management and assessment cycles and other related issues that need further clarifications.*	*Johan*	*All team members.*
90 days	*Discuss with Direct Manager on the department's top three issues and agree on monitoring process.*	*Johan*	*Direct Manager.*
90 days	*Scrub pipelines in the weekly sales meeting.*	*Johan*	*All team members.*
90 days	*Follow up on the progress of the adoption of the new sales approach based on David's best practices on a weekly basis.*	*Johan*	*All team members.*

Time	Activities	Ownership	Attendees
90 days	*Follow up on the progress of coaching the 20% to prioritize and execute on a weekly basis.*	*Johan*	*Identified 20% of team members.*
90 days	*Follow up on the progress of sourcing for skilled resources on a weekly basis.*	*Johan*	*Head of Consulting and Premier Support..*

ENDNOTES

1. John P. Kotter, *John P. Kotter on What Leaders Really Do* (Boston: Harvard Business School Press,1999), p. 51

2. John P. Kotter, *John P. Kotter on What Leaders Really Do* (Boston: Harvard Business School Press, 1999), p. 51

3. Ian Clampett, July 5th,2012, posted on Golden Foot, "Sir Alex: Perhaps the Greatest Manager of All Time," *Golden Foot Blog,* http://goldenfoot.com/sir-alex-perhaps-the-greatest-manager-of-all-time/

4. Sportsmail reporter, "As time goes on, the more I fall in love with Fergie,' admits smitten Ancelotti," *Dailymail,* October 3rd, 2011, accessed September 8th, 2012. http://www.dailymail.co.uk/sport/football/article-2044745/Carlo-Ancelotti-loves-Sir-Alex-Ferguson.html#ixzz25qUnl89J

5. Daniel Goleman, *Harvard Business Review on What Makes A Leader* (Boston: Harvard Business School Press, 2001) p. 1

6. John P. Kotter, *John P. Kotter on What Leaders Really Do* (Boston: Harvard Business School Press,1999), p. 51

7. Stephen R Covey, *The Seven Habits of Highly Effective People* (New York: Free Press, 2004) p. 151

8. "Definition of Vision," Business Dictionary, accessed July 26th,2012, http://www.businessdictionary.com/definition/vision-statement. html

9. "Definition of Strategic Objective," Business Dictionary, accessed July 26th,2012, http://www.businessdictionary.com/definition/ strategic-objective.html

10. "Definition of Critical Success Factor," Business Dictionary, http:// www.businessdictionary.com/definition/critical-success-factors-CSF. html

11. Kathy Rebello, Amy Cortese and Rob Hof, "Inside Microsoft: The Untold Story of how the Internet Forced Bill Gates to Reverse Course," *Business Week,* updated June 14th,1997, accessed July 26th,2012, http://www.businessweek.com/1996/29/b34841.htm

12. Kathy Rebello, Amy Cortese and Rob Hof, "Inside Microsoft: The Untold Story of how the Internet Forced Bill Gates to Reverse Course," *Business Week,* updated June 14th,1997, accessed July 26th,2012,

BIBLIOGRAPHY

Cohen, William A. *A Class with Drucker*. New York: Amacom, 2008.

Covey, Stephen R. *The 7 Habits of Highly Effective People*. New York: Free Press, 2004

Goleman, Daniel. *Working with Emotional Intelligence*. London: Bloomsbury Publishing Plc, 1999.

Harvard Business Review. *What Makes a Leader*. Boston: Harvard Business School Press, 2001.

Hill, Linda A. *Becoming a Manager: Mastery of a New Identity*. Boston: Harvard Business School Press, 1992

Hoyle, Mike and Newman, Peter. *Simply a Great Manager: The Fundamentals of Being a Successful Manager*. London: Marshall Cavendish Business, 2011

Kotter, John P. *John P Korter on What Leaders Really Do*. Boston: Harvard Business School Press, 1999